CSS Framework Alternatives

Explore Five Lightweight Alternatives to Bootstrap and Foundation with Project Examples

Aravind Shenoy
Anirudh Prabhu

CSS Framework Alternatives

Aravind Shenoy
Mumbai, Maharashtra, India

Anirudh Prabhu
Mumbai, India

ISBN-13 (pbk): 978-1-4842-3398-6
https://doi.org/10.1007/978-1-4842-3399-3

ISBN-13 (electronic): 978-1-4842-3399-3

Library of Congress Control Number: 2018936183

Managing Director, Apress Media LLC: Welmoed Spahr
Acquisitions Editor: Louise Corrigan
Development Editor: James Markham
Coordinating Editor: Nancy Chen

Cover designed by eStudioCalamar

Cover image designed by Freepik (www.freepik.com)

Distributed to the book trade worldwide by Springer Science+Business Media New York, 233 Spring Street, 6th Floor, New York, NY 10013. Phone 1-800-SPRINGER, fax (201) 348-4505, e-mail orders-ny@springer-sbm.com, or visit www.springeronline.com. Apress Media, LLC is a California LLC and the sole member (owner) is Springer Science + Business Media Finance Inc (SSBM Finance Inc). SSBM Finance Inc is a **Delaware** corporation.

For information on translations, please e-mail rights@apress.com, or visit www.apress.com/rights-permissions.

Apress titles may be purchased in bulk for academic, corporate, or promotional use. eBook versions and licenses are also available for most titles. For more information, reference our Print and eBook Bulk Sales web page at www.apress.com/bulk-sales.

Any source code or other supplementary material referenced by the author in this book is available to readers on GitHub via the book's product page, located at www.apress.com/9781484233986. For more detailed information, please visit www.apress.com/source-code.

Printed on acid-free paper

I dedicate this book to my uncle, R.N. Kamath,
and my sister, Aruna; without them, I am incomplete.

—Aravind Shenoy

I dedicate this to my mother and father for their
endless support and words of encouragement.
I also dedicate this to my many friends who have
supported me throughout the process. I will always
appreciate all they have done.

—Anirudh Prabhu

Table of Contents

About the Authors

Aravind Shenoy A marketing expert by profession, Aravind's core interests are technical writing, content writing, content development, web design, and business analysis. He was born and raised in Mumbai and still resides there. A music buff, he loves listening to rock 'n' roll and rap. Oasis, R.E.M., The Doors, Dire Straits, Coldplay, Jimi Hendrix, and Michael Jackson rule his playlists.

He firmly believes in this motto: "We are here for a good time, not a long time. Be happy perennially."

Anirudh Prabhu A UI developer with more than seven years of experience, Anirudh specializes in HTML, CSS, JavaScript, jQuery, Sass, LESS, Twitter, and Bootstrap. He also has experience with CoffeeScript and AngularJS.

Anirudh has worked as a technical reviewer for Apress and Packt and has been involved in building training material about HTML, CSS, and jQuery for Twenty19, which is a portal for students and interns.

About the Technical Reviewer

 **Ferit Topcu** is a software developer who has spent the last few years working and exploring the Web and JavaScript. He's been in web development for more than five years and has worked in different areas including research topics, social media analytics, and the Internet of Things. He recently joined one of Europe's biggest e-commerce companies, Zalando. At Zalando, he is developing web applications to improve its whole retail process.

Ferit has a master's degree in computer engineering from TU Berlin and is a father of two. His free time is spent with family and friends and contributing to open source projects.

Acknowledgments

As I stride through this journey of life, I want to take this opportunity to thank every person who has stood by me, especially those who believed in me when others said "Don't encourage him." Well, life is like that, and indeed life is beautiful. It couldn't have been better. Thanks to everyone who provided the right support when I needed it the most.

—Aravind Shenoy

CHAPTER 1

Choosing Lightweight Frameworks for Intuitive Web Design

When it comes to web design, Bootstrap, Foundation, and Materialize are probably the first frameworks that come to a designer's mind, given their massive range of components and attributes. However, when talking about light web projects, you do not usually need a comprehensive framework like Bootstrap or Foundation (again, depending on the complexity of your project). Usually, to build a small web site, lightweight frameworks can do the job effectively and cut down the bulk, or noise, associated with massive frameworks. For example, if your web site merely needs something like a grid or some popular components commonly found in most frameworks, then you should consider a lightweight framework.

Moreover, developing web sites and web applications from scratch is quite a tedious process as it involves writing a sizeable amount of code. Maintaining that code while the web site evolves adds to the complexity. Coding from scratch (as we like to call it) is quite an endeavor, and a framework can help you write a few lines of code and incorporate reusable sets of commonly used code that you can maintain quite easily. Clean coding and upkeep are tasks easily achieved using a framework.

© Aravind Shenoy and Anirudh Prabhu 2018
A. Shenoy and A. Prabhu, *CSS Framework Alternatives*,
https://doi.org/10.1007/978-1-4842-3399-3_1

Therefore, to simplify your web designing tasks, using a Cascading Style Sheets (CSS) framework is a good option. As mentioned earlier, there are plenty of frameworks on the Web other than Bootstrap, Foundation, and Materialize. These light frameworks are quite streamlined and remarkable, given their resourcefulness. The adage "Good things come in small packages" is applicable here.

In this chapter, we explain what frameworks are and introduce the popular Bootstrap, Foundation, and Materialize. Then we will review five lightweight frameworks: Skeleton, Milligram, UIkit, Material Design Lite, and Susy. These frameworks will be used throughout the book to build interactive and immersive web pages. In doing so, you'll form a strong basis to select the one that best suits your development needs.

What Are Frameworks?

A *framework* is a premeditated set of concepts, modules, and standardized criteria that make the task of developing web sites and web applications easier. It provides generic functionality with already written modules and tailored components created in a standard manner. In short, it is a reusable software environment that allows web designers and developers to easily build their projects and solutions with minimal coding and without worrying about the low-level details. This reduces development time and provides easy upkeep and alterations whenever necessary.

Usually, there are two kinds of frameworks.

- Front-end frameworks (CSS and JavaScript frameworks)
- Back-end or server-side programming frameworks

While back-end frameworks are used by web developers and programmers to build applications on the server-side, front-end frameworks are used by web designers and developers for implementing the Cascading Style Sheets language.

In this book, you will get a glimpse into front-end frameworks, which basically are pre-prepared packages containing the structure of files and folders of Hypertext Markup Language (HTML) and CSS documents (some with JavaScript functions), which help designers and developers build interactive and immersive web sites.

Frameworks allow you to use a common standardized structure that cuts out much of the groundwork of writing code from scratch and helps you reuse components, modules, and libraries, freeing you up to focus on core tasks at a high level.

Components of a CSS Framework

The following are the basic components of a CSS framework:

- Grids (structures that help organize the content and design the layout)

- Typography elements

- Cross-browser compatibility

- Helper classes for positioning elements

- Utility classes

- Navigational elements

- Source code written in preprocessors such as Sass and LESS

- Media elements (badges, tooltips, comments, and so on)

3

Advantages of Using a CSS Framework

Though some people have advocated not using CSS frameworks, mainly because of issues such as bloated structure, ingrained HTML markup, and a common aesthetic across framework-based web sites, using a CSS framework has several benefits. You should try using a CSS framework for the following reasons:

- Clean and consistent coding

- Cross-browser compatibility

- Grid-based design

- The ability to incorporate healthy coding practices

- Easy-to-build prototypes

- Easy maintenance and upkeep

- Allows reuse and clean homogenous code structure

- Easy expandability and modifications

- Solid documentation

- Common ground for building immersive web sites

- Accessibility

A budding developer can find it difficult to build web sites just based on pure HTML, CSS, and JavaScript. In addition, grid-based layouts help budding designers to position, structure, and design the layout quite easily. You do not have to reinvent the wheel, meaning you can get some hands-on experience without the intricacies and dilemmas that you will come across when you code from scratch. Good and clean coding practices are imperative when you grow as a web designer, and frameworks are all about awesome cohesiveness and consistent coding that will hold you in good stead in times to come.

Various Popular Frameworks

In this section, you will look at the most popular frameworks used by web designers across the globe. The most popular frameworks for designing web sites are Bootstrap, Foundation, and Materialize. Which one a developer chooses depends on the needs and requirements of a web site and its design. However, just because a framework is popular doesn't mean it fits the bill when it comes to designing your projects. You need to consider several issues when it comes to selecting a framework; we'll talk more about that later. Let's now take a look at the various superlative frameworks that are in vogue today.

Bootstrap

Bootstrap is the most popular mobile-first framework in web design; it's used extensively by developers across the globe (Figure 1-1). You can find more information on the official web site at `http://getbootstrap.com/`.

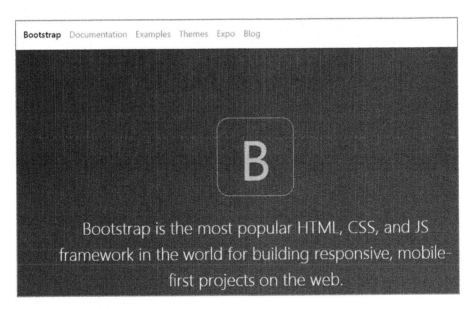

Figure 1-1. *Bootstrap*

Bootstrap adopts a mobile-first paradigm by which you can build responsive web sites. It comes with components, modules, JavaScript functions, and media queries that help developers build immersive web sites with ease.

Foundation

Foundation was the earliest responsive framework and is as massive and advanced as Bootstrap for building web products and services (Figure 1-2). Foundation comes with cool features such as Flex Grid and Motion UI. The latest version, Foundation 6, is quicker, is lighter in size compared to its earlier versions, and is a solid front-end framework for designing beautiful web sites, e-mails, and apps that look good on any device. You can find more information on the official web site at `http://foundation.zurb.com/`.

Figure 1-2. *Foundation*

Materialize

Materialize is a modern front-end framework based on Google's Material Design philosophy that helps developers build and design immersive web sites (Figure 1-3). You can find more information on the official web site at `http://materializecss.com/`.

Figure 1-3. *Materialize*

Materialize has a superlative, creative user interface (UI) component library that incorporates cross-browser compatibility and device-agnostic capabilities for developing attractive and consistent web sites.

Skeleton

As mentioned earlier, sometimes you don't need a large framework, especially if you are embarking on a small project. Skeleton is a simple, responsive boilerplate and is extremely lightweight with 400 lines of code and with a mobile-based philosophy (Figure 1-4). You can find more information on the official web site at `http://getskeleton.com/`.

A dead simple, responsive boilerplate.

DOWNLOAD

Light as a feather at ~400 lines & built with mobile in mind.

Styles designed to be a starting point, not a UI framework.

Quick to start with zero compiling or installing necessary.

Figure 1-4. *Skeleton*

Milligram

Milligram is a minimalistic framework with just enough styles for small and interactive web sites (Figure 1-5). Its zipped file size is only 2KB. It comes with a mobile-first philosophy and supports the modern browser versions of Chrome, Firefox, Safari, IE, and Opera. Its cutting-edge features include the FlexBox grid system, and it is a simple, top-notch framework from a usability point of view. You can find more information on the official web site at `http://milligram.io/`.

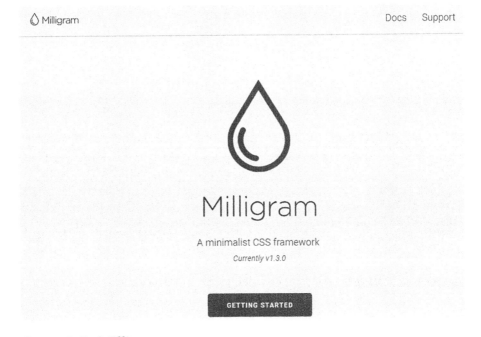

Figure 1-5. *Milligram*

UIkit

UIkit is a light and modular front-end framework for developing faster and powerful web interfaces (Figure 1-6). It has a massive collection of HTML, CSS, and JavaScript components and modules that can be extended with themes. It is flexible because it can be customized to give a unique feel to your web sites. You can find more information on the official web site at `https://getuikit.com/v2/`.

Figure 1-6. *UIkit*

Material Design Lite

Google released its own front-end framework called Material Design Lite (MDL) that is based on its Material Design philosophy (Figure 1-7). MDL is a lightweight framework with few dependencies and is focused on simple web sites such as blogs and landing pages. It allows you to customize styles and web sites designed using MDL degrade gracefully in legacy browsers. You can find more information on the official web site at `https://getmdl.io/`.

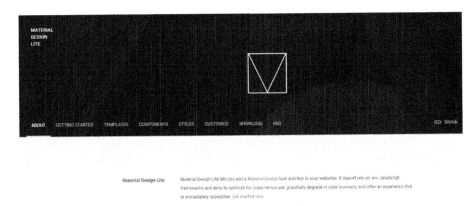

Figure 1-7. *Material Design Lite*

Susy

In today's era of agile development and constant changes, the layout designs are crucial and cannot be restricted to a single framework, especially if your web site is intricate design-wise. With Susy (Figure 1-8), the settings are not set in stone, meaning you can use its integrated Sass-based libraries to create immersive layouts with potent structural designs. Susy is not a typical framework but more of a UI utility as it simplifies and streamlines the task of designing intricate grid layouts. You can find more information on the official web site at `http://susy.oddbird.net/`.

11

Power tools for the web

YOUR MARKUP, YOUR DESIGN, YOUR OPINIONS | *OUR MATH*.

In a world of agile development and super-tablet-multi-magic-laptop-phones, the best layouts can't be contained in a single framework or technique. CSS Libraries are a bloated mess of opinions about how to do your job. Why let the table-saw tell you where to put the kitchen?

Figure 1-8. Susy

Choosing a Framework

As you can see, we have covered many popular frameworks. Choosing the right framework is quite important and depends on the needs and requirement of your projects. Some frameworks are bloated, meaning they have too many built-in styles, which might not be required for a small project.

The following are some of the factors that you should consider when choosing a framework:

- An existing web project may already be using a particular framework that cannot be used with your desired framework.

- Some projects may not need the clutter associated with heavyweight frameworks for performance-related issues.

- You might need different preprocessor support such as for LESS or Sass, which is not integrated with your desired framework.

- Web sites built with a particular framework may look similar if not customized to give them an authentic look and feel.

There are several other factors such as the ease of use, speed of configuration, usability, features, widgets, components, long-term support, and reliability that you need to consider when choosing a framework. In summary, you need to choose your framework based on the requirements and needs of the project; especially when choosing lightweight front-end kits for small projects, given the bloat and bulk associated with massive frameworks.

Concept of Grids

A grid system allows you to structure and stack content horizontally and vertically in an easy manner. It is easily adaptable for any web site or web application and has a lot of advantages. It is usually responsive, meaning it adjusts itself based on the browser or device width. So, it displays the content appropriately in a mobile device, a laptop, a tablet, or a desktop depending on the size of the device. Plus, you have media queries, which help you define the grid layout based on the device width.

Grids are usually 12-column containers in many frameworks but can be customized using methods specific to the framework. You can have flexible layouts wherein you can divide the page into several regions and place content using the markup.

Another concept catching on in CSS designs is the FlexBox. The difference between a grid and FlexBox layout is that grid layouts are two-dimensional, while a FlexBox is usually one-dimensional wherein you can lay out content in a row or a column.

The choice of using a grid layout or a FlexBox depends on how you want to structure your content. With a FlexBox you space out the content and build a structure using that content. Suppose you have certain items; it is up to you to decide how much space each item should take. Grid layouts, on the other hand, are content-agnostic. In grid layouts, you create a layout and place the content into rows and columns.

In most modern frameworks, both the grid and the FlexBox are supported. While the usability of the grid layout is awesome, a FlexBox can help you place things more aesthetically.

For a detailed explanation of the grid concept, you can refer the Mozilla developer network web site, specifically the following web page, for in-depth information: `https://developer.mozilla.org/en-US/docs/ Web/CSS/CSS_Grid_Layout`.

Summary

In this chapter, we gave you an overview of some popular CSS frameworks. We also covered the benefits of using a CSS framework. CSS frameworks are comprised of components, modules, libraries, navigational elements, typography, media queries, tailor-made widgets, and grid layouts that make web design a breeze. We also gave you an overview of grid and FlexBox layouts.

We will now dedicate a chapter for each of the frameworks mentioned in the introduction of the chapter, starting with Skeleton. With each chapter, we use a progressive approach, meaning the next framework is more extensive and a framework's resourcefulness increases as you move through the book.

CHAPTER 2

Building a Landing Page with Skeleton

Skeleton is an intuitive framework for lightweight projects. It is extremely lightweight with a handful of HTML elements and was developed with a mobile-first philosophy. In this chapter, you will learn how to install Skeleton. You will also learn about its grid system and attributes; Finally, we will build a landing web page with Skeleton.

Installing Skeleton

To get started, go to the Skeleton web site at `http://getskeleton.com/`. You will see the Download button, which is highlighted in a red box in Figure 2-1.

© Aravind Shenoy and Anirudh Prabhu 2018
A. Shenoy and A. Prabhu, *CSS Framework Alternatives*,
https://doi.org/10.1007/978-1-4842-3399-3_2

A dead simple, responsive boilerplate.

Light as a feather at ~400 lines &
built with mobile in mind.

Styles designed to be a starting
point, not a UI framework.

Quick to start with zero compiling
or installing necessary.

Figure 2-1. *Skeleton download page*

Click Download to download the Skeleton `.zip` file. After unzipping the file, you will see the file structure shown in Figure 2-2.

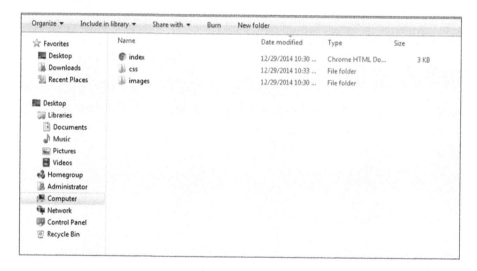

Figure 2-2. *Content of the Skeleton framework*

The `css` folder is where you save your CSS files. By default, the `css` folder contains the Normalize and Skeleton style sheets.

Normalize.css is a small CSS file that provides better cross-browser consistency in the default styling of HTML elements. It makes browsers render all elements more consistently and in line with modern standards. It precisely targets only the styles that need normalizing. You can find more information about Normalize on the official web site at https://necolas. github.io/normalize.css/.

You can also see the images folder where you can store your images. By default, the images folder contains the favicon image for Skeleton.

The index.html file is your default web page. When you edit the page in Notepad++ or any editor, you will see the code displayed in Listing 2-1.

Listing 2-1. Basic Skeleton Example

```
<!DOCTYPE html>
<html lang="en">
<head>

  <!-- Basic Page Needs ------------------------------------- -->
  <meta charset="utf-8">
  <title>Your page title here :)</title>
  <meta name="description" content="">
  <meta name="author" content="">

  <!-- Mobile Specific Metas ------------------------------- -->
  <meta name="viewport" content="width=device-width,
  initial-scale=1">

  <!-FONT  ---------------------------------------------- -->
  <link href="//fonts.googleapis.com/css?family=
  Raleway:400,300,600" rel="stylesheet" type="text/css">

  <!-CSS  ----------------------------------------------- -->
  <link rel="stylesheet" href="css/normalize.css">
  <link rel="stylesheet" href="css/skeleton.css">
```

```
    <!—Favicon  ------------------------------------------- -->
    <link rel="icon" type="image/png" href="images/favicon.png">

</head>
<body>

    <!-- Primary Page Layout ------------------------------- -->
    <div class="container">
      <div class="row">
        <div class="one-half column" style="margin-top: 25%">
          <h4>Basic Page</h4>
          <p>This index.html page is a placeholder with the
          CSS, font and favicon. It's just waiting for you
          to add some content! If you need some help hit up
          the <a href="http://www.getskeleton.com">Skeleton
          documentation</a>.</p>
        </div>
      </div>
    </div>

<!-- End Document ------------------------------------------- -->
</body>
</html>
```

Now click the index.html file to display the web page, as shown in Figure 2-3.

Basic Page

This index.html page is a placeholder with the CSS, font and favicon.
It's just waiting for you to add some content! If you need some help hit
up the Skeleton documentation.

Figure 2-3. *Skeleton basic example in a browser*

Skeleton's Grid System

Like most other frameworks, Skeleton has its own grid system. It is
essentially a 12-column grid with a maximum width of 960px. It is a
responsive grid that adjusts itself depending on the browser/device size.

Take a look at the code snippet in Listing 2-2 to understand how the
grid system works.

Listing 2-2. Skeleton Grid System Demonstrated

```
<body>
<div class="container">
<!-- columns should be the immediate child of a .row -->
        <div class="row">
                <div style="text-align:center; border: 1px
                solid black;" class="one column">One</div>
                <div style="text-align:center; border:
                1px solid black;" class="eleven
                columns">Eleven</div>
        </div>
```

```html
<br>
  <!-- just use a number and class 'column' or 'columns' -->
    <div class="row">
            <div style="text-align:center; border: 1px solid
            black;" class="two columns">Two</div>
            <div style="text-align:center; border: 1px solid
            black;" class="ten columns">Ten</div>
    </div>
<br>

    <div class="row">
            <div style="text-align:center; border: 1px solid
            black;" class="three columns">Three</div>
            <div style="text-align:center; border: 1px solid
            black;" class="nine columns">Nine</div>
    </div>
<br>

    <div class="row">
            <div style="text-align:center; border: 1px solid
            black;" class="four columns">Four</div>
            <div style="text-align:center; border: 1px solid
            black;" class="eight columns">Ten</div>
    </div>
<br>

    <div class="row">
            <div style="text-align:center; border: 1px solid
            black;" class="five columns">Five</div>
            <div style="text-align:center; border: 1px solid
            black;" class="seven columns">Seven</div>
    </div>
```

```
<br>
    <div class="row">
        <div style="text-align:center; border: 1px solid
        black;" class="six columns">Six</div>
        <div style="text-align:center; border: 1px solid
        black;" class="six columns">Six</div>
    </div>
<br>
    <div class="row">
        <div style="text-align:center; border: 1px solid
        black;" class="seven columns">Seven</div>
        <div style="text-align:center; border: 1px solid
        black;" class="five columns">Five</div>
    </div>
<br>
    <div class="row">
        <div style="text-align:center; border: 1px solid
        black;" class="eight columns">Eight</div>
        <div style="text-align:center; border: 1px solid
        black;" class="four columns">Four</div>
    </div>
<br>
    <div class="row">
        <div style="text-align:center; border: 1px solid
        black;" class="nine columns">Nine</div>
        <div style="text-align:center; border: 1px solid
        black;" class="three columns">Three</div>
    </div>
```

```
<br>
    <div class="row">
        <div style="text-align:center; border: 1px solid
        black;" class="ten columns">Ten</div>
        <div style="text-align:center; border: 1px solid
        black;" class="two columns">Two</div>
    </div>
<br>
    <div class="row">
        <div style="text-align:center; border: 1px solid
        black;" class="eleven columns">Eleven</div>
        <div style="text-align:center; border: 1px solid
        black;" class="one columns">One</div>
    </div>
<br>
    </div
  </div>

<!-- End Document ---------------------------------------- -->
</body>
```

In Listing 2-2, you define a <body> element within which you define a
<div> with the container class. Inside that, you define the <div> with the
row class. Within that <div>, you define two <div>s, one with a column
width of one column and other with a column width of eleven columns.

Remember that the <div> with the column classes should be the
immediate child of the <div> with the row class. To define one column,
you use the one column class. Similarly, to define eleven columns, you use
the eleven columns class. For two columns, the class is two columns.

Note that you use an inline CSS style of `<style="text-align:center;` `border: 1px solid black;">` with each column to align the text in the center and dedicate a black border of 1px for each column. You use the `<br>` element for spacing between each row.

Basically, the code in Listing 2-2 defines different rows with a `<div>` class and defines columns of different widths. Figure 2-4 shows the output of the code on execution.

One	Eleven

Two	Ten

Three	Nine

Four	Ten

Five	Seven

Six	Six

Seven	Five

Eight	Four

Nine	Three

Ten	Two

Eleven	One

Figure 2-4. Skeleton grid system demonstrated

As you can see in Figure 2-4, the first row has two columns defined with widths of one and eleven columns, respectively. The second row has two columns with widths of two and ten columns, respectively. Similarly, you define eleven rows each with two columns of varying widths.

Now you have an idea how the grid system works in Skeleton.

An Overview of Skeleton's Attributes

Let's take a look at some attributes of the Skeleton framework.

- Skeleton's typography base is Raleway, a Google-based typography. The font size defaults to HTML's font sizes, and the typography retains properties such as anchors, strong, emphasis, and underline similar to HTML's basic typography.

- Buttons in Skeleton can be created using the `button-primary` class, which is easily distinguishable. You can also opt for standard buttons if you don't want enhanced buttons. For that, instead of `button-primary`, you just have to use the `button` class. You can also define a button using the `<button>` element or use an anchor tag, `<a>`, with the `button` or `button-primary` class.

- Unordered lists in Skeleton can be created using the `<ul>` class. If you want to use a numbered list, you can use the `<ol>` class.

- Code styling can be set by using the `<code>` class. For several blocks of code, you can use the `<code>` element within a `<pre>` element.

- Tables in Skeleton are similar to HTML tables where you use the `<thead>` and `<tbody>` elements. Similar to HTML, you use `<tr>` to define the table rows, `<td>` for the table data, and `<th>` for the table heading; you wrap everything within the main `<table>` element.

- Skeleton uses mobile-first queries, which target the minimum width. Styles outside of a query apply to all devices. This is done to prevent small devices such as phones and tablets from parsing loads of unused CSS.

- Skeleton uses the following media query sizes based on the device size:
    - *Mobile*: 400px
    - *Phablet*: 550px
    - *Tablet*: 750px
    - *Desktop*: 1000px
    - *Desktop HD*: 1200px

Skeleton also comes with many helper classes that can be used to limit the elements within a container, float the element to the left or right, and clear the floats on both sides.

Building a Landing Web Page with Skeleton

In this section, you will create a landing page for a freelance portal called RemoteDesk. The landing page shows the various things you can do on the freelance portal. You will design a web page that shows several aspects of the freelance portal along with company information and other basic features.

We will divide the process of building the web page into six Steps. After these six Steps, you will have a complete landing page.

Step 1: Defining the Content Area

You will define the <html> tags and then move on to include the necessary links for Skeleton and Normalize (included by default in Skeleton) and the custom style sheet in the <head> tags (more about that in the code explanation). Then you will define the <body> section after the <head> tags and within the <html> tags. Inside the <body> tags, you will define the <div> class with the necessary rows and columns with the required content. Essentially, each content area will be encapsulated in an element with the row class. Depending on the content, you will divide the area into sections using elements with the columns class in that section's parent row.

Let's look at Listing 2-3.

Listing 2-3. Defining the Content Area

```
<html>
    <head>
        <!-- Step1: Include the necessary style and heading-->
        <meta name="viewport" content="width=device-width,
        initial-scale=1.0,maximum-scale=1.0"/>
        <link href="https://fonts.googleapis.com/
        css?family=Source+Sans+Pro" rel="stylesheet">
        <link href="css/normalize.css" rel="stylesheet"
        type="text/css"/>
        <link href="css/skeleton.css" rel="stylesheet"
        type="text/css"/>
        <link href="css/style.css"  rel="stylesheet"
        type="text/css"/>
        <title>Best Freelance management app</title>
        <!-- end of Step 1-->
    </head>
    <body class="container">
        <!-- Navigation area -->
        <div class="row">
            <div class="two columns logo">RemoteDesk.com</div>
            <div class="eight columns"> </div>
            <div class="two columns">
                <a class="button button-primary" href="#">Sign
                up</a>
            </div>
```

```
    </div>
    <!-- Navigation area ends -->
  </body>
</html>
```

As you can see in Listing 2-3, you define the viewport size inside the head section. A *viewport* controls the way a web page is displayed on a mobile device. If you do not use a viewport, a mobile device will render the page in a typical desktop screen width. Setting a viewport helps you exercise control over a page's width and scaling on varied devices.

You can find more about viewports at https://developers.google.com/speed/docs/insights/ConfigureViewport.

Then, by default in Skeleton, you set the links for Normalize and Skeleton. Remember that if the path to your files is different, you need to specify so. For now, they should be in the root folder, so the default path is good to go. Then you define the path for the custom style sheet called as style.css, which you will place in the css folder. You define a <body> tag and assign the container class to it. The container is the main centered wrapper. You define a <div> element and assign a row class to it.

Inside that <div> element, you define three <div>s. The first <div> contains the content RemoteDesk.com and spans two columns.

The next <div> spans eight columns, and you assign the   value between the <div> tags. Essentially,   creates a *nonbreaking* space. It is used in programming and web design to create a space in a line that cannot be broken with word wrap. Using it will help create multiple spaces that are visible on a web page and not only in the source code.

(We are using this because there are no offset classes in Skeleton compared to other frameworks like Bootstrap and Foundation.)

The third <div> spans two columns and contains the Sign Up button, which we create using the button-primary class.

Figure 2-5 shows the output of the code.

RemoteDesk.com

Figure 2-5. *The output of the content area*

Step 2: Completing the <body> Tag Content

Now, you will create the rest of the content within the <body> tags.

You will start with inserting an image, as shown in Listing 2-4. (Refer to the entire code in the code bundle to see the positioning of the various elements; we have included code in steps in the code bundle so that you can have a better understanding of each step. Finally, index.html contains the entire code for the landing page.)

Listing 2-4. Inserting the Header Image

```
<div class="row masthead"></div>
```

You have just used the row class and assigned a class called masthead to it. The image is defined in the code in the style sheet called Style.css. The image referred to, masthead.png, is located in the images folder where you will keep all the images.

In style.css, you define the code, as shown in Listing 2-5.

Listing 2-5. Inserting Header Image

```
.masthead{
    background: url("../images/masthead.png") no-repeat center;
    height: 462px;
    background-size: cover;
}
```

Remember that the code shown in Listing 2-5 is the code in the custom CSS style sheet called style.css.

You assign a height of 462px and center the image. You also assign the value cover to the background-size property; this scales the background image to be as large as possible so that the background area is fully covered by the image.

Now on executing the index.html page, you will get the output shown in Figure 2-6.

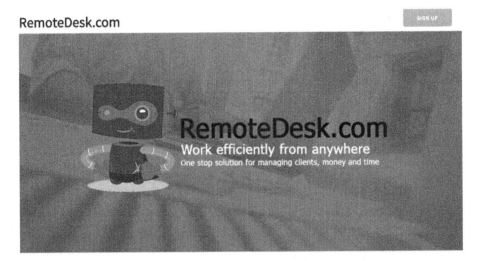

Figure 2-6. *Output of the header image*

Step 3: Defining the Freelance Portal

Next, you will create a later section of the page where you define the features of the freelance portal. To create this section, let's look at the code snippet shown in Listing 2-6.

Listing 2-6. Defining the Content Area for the "Rewarding" Section

```
<div class="row rewardingContent">
        <div class="six columns">
            <h3>Plenty of rewarding projects</h3>
```

```
        <p>RemoteDesk is a great place to find more
        clients, and to run and grow your own freelance
        business.</p>
        <ul>
            <li><strong>Freedom to work on ideal
            projects.</strong> On RemoteDesk, you run
            your own business and choose your own
            clients and projects. Just complete your
            profile and we'll highlight ideal jobs.
            Also search projects, and respond to client
            invitations.</li>
            <li><strong>Wide variety and high pay.
            </strong> Clients are now posting jobs in
            hundreds of skill categories, paying top
            price for great work.</li>
            <li><strong>More and more success.
            </strong> The greater the success you have
            on projects, the more likely you are to get
            hired by clients that use Upwork.</li>
        </ul>
    </div>
    <div class="six columns">
        <img src="images/medal.png"
        class="rewardingImg"/>
    </div>
</div>
```

In Listing 2-6, you create another `<div>` with the row class. You also assign a `rewardingContent` custom class to it. Then, you divide the section of the page into two rows each spanning six columns in width.
The first `<div>` within the `<div>` with the row class is assigned a width of six columns using the `six columns` class. You assign a heading inside it.

You create a list using the `<ul>` tags and define the list items using the `<li>` tags. Then, you create the second `<div>` spanning six columns where you insert an image using the `<img>` tag. You also add a custom `rewardingImg` class to it.

Next, you can see what to do with the custom classes, `rewardingContent` and `rewardingImg`, in the `style.css` style sheet, as shown in Listing 2-7.

Listing 2-7. Defining Styles Related to the "Rewarding" Section

```
.rewardingContent {
    margin-top:10px;
}
.rewardingImg {
    width: 75%;
    margin: 0 auto;
    display: block;
}
```

In this code, you add a margin to the `rewardingContent` class to set the whitespace around the border. You use the `display: block` for the `rewardingImg` so that it occupies the space of the parent element. (You need to use the `display: block` property because Skeleton does not have any utility classes for responsive images.) You also define a width for the image and center it using `margin: 0 auto`.

Figure 2-7 shows the later section of the page as created in Step 3.

Plenty of rewarding projects

RemoteDesk is a great place to find more clients, and to run and grow
your own freelance business.

○   **Freedom to work on ideal projects.** On RemoteDesk, you run your
own business and choose your own clients and projects. Just complete
your profile and we'll highlight ideal jobs. Also search projects, and
respond to client invitations.

○   **Wide variety and high pay.** Clients are now posting jobs in hundreds
of skill categories, paying top price for great work.

○   **More and more success.** The greater the success you have on
projects, the more likely you are to get hired by clients that use Upwork.

Figure 2-7. *Output of the "rewarding" section*

Step 4: Completing the Sections

Next, you will create the remaining three sections using the code in
Listing 2-8.

Listing 2-8. Adding Content to the Remaining Sections

```
<div class="row hiredContent">
        <div class="six columns">
            <img src="images/hire-resources-icon.png"
            class="hiringImg"/>
        </div>
        <div class="six columns">
            <h3>Get hired quickly</h3>
            <p>RemoteDesk makes it easy to connect with
            clients and begin doing great work.</p>
            <ul>
                <li><strong>Streamlined hiring.</strong>
                RemoteDesk's sophisticated algorithms highlight
                projects you're a great fit for.</li>
```

```
        <li><strong>Top Rated and Rising Talent
        programs.</strong> Enjoy higher visibility
        with the added status of prestigious
        programs.</li>
        <li><strong>Do substantial work with top
        clients.</strong> RemoteDesk pricing
        encourages freelancers to use Upwork for
        repeat relationships with their clients.</li>
    </ul>
  </div>
</div>
<!-- Hired content end -->
<!-- work efficiency start-->
<div class="row workEfficiency">
    <div class="six columns">
        <h3>Work efficiently, effectively.</h3>
        <p>With Upwork, you have the freedom and
        flexibility to control when, where, and how you
        work. Each project includes an online workspace
        shared by you and your client, allowing you
        to:</p>
        <ul>
            <li><strong>Send and receive files.
            </strong> Deliver digital assets in a secure
            environment.</li>
            <li><strong>Share feedback in real time.
            </strong> Use Upwork Messages to communicate
            via text, chat, or video.</li>
```

```
            <li><strong>Use our mobile app.</strong> Many
            features can be accessed on your mobile phone
            when on the go.</li>
        </ul>
    </div>
    <div class="six columns">
        <img src="images/Messaging.png"
        class="messagingImg"/>
    </div>
</div>
<!-- Work efficiency end-->
<!-- Get paid section start -->
<div class="row getPaid">
    <div class="six columns"><img src="images/paid.png"
    class="paidImg"/></div>
    <div class="six columns">
        <h3>Get paid on time</h3>
        <p>All projects include Upwork Payment
        Protection – helping ensure that you get paid
        for all work successfully completed through the
        freelancing website.</p>
        <ul>
            <li><strong>All invoices and payments happen
            through RemoteDesk.</strong> Count on a
            simple and streamlined process.</li>
            <li><strong>Hourly and fixed-price
            projects. For hourly work, submit
            timesheets through RemoteDesk.</strong> For
            fixed-price jobs, set milestones and funds
            are released via Upwork escrow features.
            </strong>
```

```
<li><strong>Multiple payment options.
</strong> Choose a payment method that works
best for you, from direct deposit or PayPal
to wire transfer and more.</li>
    </ul>
  </div>
</div>
```

As shown in Listing 2-8, you create three rows using three <div>s with the row class. In the first <div> containing the row class, you create two <div>s each spanning six columns. In the first child <div>, you insert an image using the <img> tag, and in the second child <div>, you create a heading followed by creating a list using the <ul> and <li> tags. In short, you create the next three content blocks using a similar technique as you did in Step 3.

Similarly, you create a similar structure for the remaining two <div>s with the row class by inserting two child <div>s, each spanning six columns. You also insert an image and create an unordered list similar to the previous <div>s.

Then, you define the CSS styles for the custom CSS code in the style.css style sheet just like you did in Step 3. Listing 2-9 shows the CSS style sheet code.

Listing 2-9. Adding Styles for the Remaining Sections

```
.rewardingContent,.hiredContent,.workEfficiency,.getPaid{
    margin-top:10px;
}
.rewardingImg,.hiringImg,.messagingImg,.paidImg {
    width: 75%;
    margin: 0 auto;
    display: block;
}
```

Figure 2-8 shows the output of the code in Step 4.

Get hired quickly

RemoteDesk makes it easy to connect with clients and begin doing great work.

- Streamlined hiring. RemoteDesk's sophisticated algorithms highlight projects you're a great fit for.

- Top Rated and Rising Talent programs. Enjoy higher visibility with the added status of prestigious programs.

- Do substantial work with top clients. RemoteDesk pricing encourages freelancers to use Upwork for repeat relationships with their clients.

Work efficiently, effectively.

With Upwork, you have the freedom and flexibility to control when, where, and how you work. Each project includes an online workspace shared by you and your client, allowing you to:

- Send and receive files. Deliver digital assets in a secure environment.

- Share feedback in real time. Use Upwork Messages to communicate via text, chat, or video.

- Use our mobile app. Many features can be accessed on your mobile phone when on the go.

Get paid on time

All projects include Upwork Payment Protection — helping ensure that you get paid for all work successfully completed through the freelancing website.

- All invoices and payments happen through RemoteDesk. Count on a simple and streamlined process.

- Hourly and fixed-price projects. For hourly work, submit timesheets through RemoteDesk. For fixed-price jobs, set milestones and funds are released via Upwork escrow features.

- Multiple payment options. Choose a payment method that works best for you, from direct deposit or PayPal to wire transfer and more.

Figure 2-8. *Output of the content of the remaining sections*

Step 5: Designing a Sign-up Form

In this Step, you will create a small sign-up form. Listing 2-10 shows the code for the form.

Listing 2-10. Sign-up Form

```
<h3 class="row">Ready to get hired?</h3>
      <div class="row quickSignup">
          <div class="five columns"><input type="text"
          name="fullName" class="fullName u-full-width"
          id="fullName" placeholder="Enter your full
          name"/></div>
          <div class="five columns"><input type="text"
          name="emailId" class="emailId u-full-width"
          id="emailId" placeholder="Enter your email"/></div>
          <div class="two columns"><a class="button button-
          primary" href="#">Sign up</a></div>
      </div>
```

In Listing 2-10, you create a `<div>` and assign the `row` class to it. You then add three `<div>`s with the `columns` class within the `<div>` with the `row` class. You then add inputs in the first two `<div>`s for the full name and e-mail. Here you use a utility class provided by Skeleton; for example, `u-full-width` is used so that the fields occupy the full width of the container. You then place a Sign Up button in the last `<div>`.

Figure 2-9 shows the output of the form.

Ready to get hired?

| Enter your full name | Enter your email | SIGN UP |

Figure 2-9. *Output of the sign-up form*

Step 6: Creating a Footer

Finally, you will create the footer. Listing 2-11 shows the code for the footer section.

Listing 2-11. Footer

```
<div class="row footer">
        <div class="four columns">
            <h4>Company Info</h4>
            <a class="column">About us</a>
            <a class="column">Customer Stories</a>
            <a class="column">Press</a>
            <a class="column">Career</a>
            <a class="column">RemoteDesk Blog</a>
            <a class="column">Terms of service</a>
            <a class="column">Privacy Policy</a>
        </div>
        <div class="four columns">
            <h4>Additional Services</h4>
            <a class="column">Enterprise Solutions</a>
            <a class="column">Enterprise Summit</a>
            <a class="column">Business resources</a>
        </div>
        <div class="four columns">
            <h4>Browse</h4>
            <a class="column">Freelancers by skills</a>
            <a class="column">Freelancers by region</a>
            <a class="column">Find Jobs</a>
            <a class="column">Hiring Resources</a>
        </div>
    </div>
```

In Listing 2-11, you create a `<div>` tag and assign a `row` class to it. Within that `<div>`, you create three child `<div>`s, each spanning four columns using the `four columns` class.

The first child `<div>` contains anchor links, `<a>`, for the company information. The second child `<div>` contains anchor links for the additional services, whereas the third child `<div>` contains anchor links for the Browse section.

Figure 2-10 shows the footer section of the web page.

Company Info	Additional Services	Browse
About us	Enterprise Solutions	Freelancers by skills
Customer Stories	Enterprise Summit	Freelancers by region
Press	Business resources	Find Jobs
Career		Hiring Resources
RemoteDesk Blog		
Terms of service		
Privacy Policy		

Figure 2-10. *Output of the footer section*

You have just designed a landing page for the RemoteDesk freelance portal using Skeleton!

Summary

Skeleton is a simple framework that beginners can adopt quickly. It has a clean and concise code base.

However, Skeleton does have its drawbacks.

- It lacks several CSS features that other frameworks provide. Because of this, the development time while using Skeleton is higher compared to its counterparts.

- The maximum width supported by the 12-column fluid grid is 960px.

- Another drawback is the lack of community support.
  The last update to this framework was done three years
  ago. Moreover, a lot of pull requests and issues are still
  open, meaning all the discrepancies have yet to be fixed
  along with substantial updates.

Therefore, when it comes to massive, immersive web sites, Skeleton falls short. Nevertheless, it is a handy utility suitable for web projects, meant mainly for smaller screens. In the next chapter, you will design a product page with Milligram, another intuitive lightweight framework.

CHAPTER 3

Building a Product Page with Milligram

Milligram is a lightweight framework for designing interactive web sites. This intuitive framework has a minimal set of styles, is apt for building web pages with high performance, and adopts the paradigm of clean and consistent coding. Its zipped file size is only 2KB, making it extremely lightweight for creating small web sites. In this chapter, you will learn how to install Milligram and about its grid feature. Then you will build a product page with the framework.

Installing Milligram

There are different ways you can install Milligram. In this section, you will learn how to install Milligram by downloading the Milligram files.

Go to the Milligram web site at `http://milligram.io/` and click the Download Milligram button, as highlighted in Figure 3-1. The zip file will be downloaded.

© Aravind Shenoy and Anirudh Prabhu 2018
A. Shenoy and A. Prabhu, *CSS Framework Alternatives*,
https://doi.org/10.1007/978-1-4842-3399-3_3

◇ Milligram   Docs   Support

Getting Started

There are some ways to get started. First, see all download options available below, then choose the most suitable option for your need. Now you should add the main file of the Milligram and the CSS Reset in the header of your project. Just that!

Figure 3-1. *Milligram download page*

Figure 3-2 shows the file structure.

.github	26-01-2017 02:02	File folder	
dist	26-01-2017 02:02	File folder	
examples	26-01-2017 02:02	File folder	
src	26-01-2017 02:02	File folder	
test	26-01-2017 02:02	File folder	
.appveyor.yml	26-01-2017 02:02	YML File	1 KB
.editorconfig	26-01-2017 02:02	EDITORCONFIG File	1 KB
.eslintrc	26-01-2017 02:02	ESLINTRC File	1 KB
.gitignore	26-01-2017 02:02	GITIGNORE File	1 KB
.sasslintrc	26-01-2017 02:02	SASSLINTRC File	2 KB
.travis.yml	26-01-2017 02:02	YML File	1 KB
backstop.conf	26-01-2017 02:02	JScript Script File	3 KB
bower.json	26-01-2017 02:02	JSON File	1 KB
changelog.md	26-01-2017 02:02	MD File	1 KB
composer.json	26-01-2017 02:02	JSON File	1 KB
license	26-01-2017 02:02	File	2 KB
package	26-01-2017 02:02	JScript Script File	1 KB
package.json	26-01-2017 02:02	JSON File	3 KB
readme.md	26-01-2017 02:02	MD File	3 KB
yarn.lock	26-01-2017 02:02	LOCK File	175 KB

Figure 3-2. *Content of the Milligram framework*

The CSS files (both the usual ones as well as the minified versions) are present in the dist folder. Figure 3-3 shows the file structure.

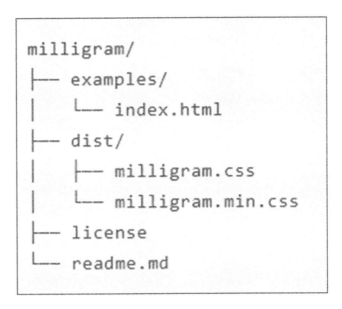

```
milligram/
├── examples/
│       └── index.html
├── dist/
│       ├── milligram.css
│       └── milligram.min.css
├── license
└── readme.md
```

Figure 3-3. *File structure of Milligram framework (source: Milligram)*

You can also download the Milligram files or install it using Bower, NPM, or Yarn.

For installation through Bower, NPM, and Yarn, you need to use the following commands from the command-line prompt:

```
$ bower install milligram
$ npm install milligram
$ yarn add milligram
```

Once you download Milligram, add the tags for the files in the head section of your HTML code.

There is a preferred way of using Milligram that we will be showing in this chapter, which is to use a content delivery network (CDN). A CDN is basically a system of distributed networks delivering web pages and other web content according to the geographic location of the users, the source of the web pages, and the location of the CDN server. There are many benefits of using CDN.

- Decreases the server load

- Enables fast content delivery

- Ensures high availability

- Facilitates high network backbone capacity for concurrency

- Offers better control of asset delivery

You can add the CDN code for Milligram using the following lines of code:

```
<link href="https://fonts.googleapis.com/css?family=Roboto"
rel="stylesheet">
<link href="https://cdnjs.cloudflare.com/ajax/libs/milligram/
1.3.0/milligram.min.css" rel="stylesheet" type="text/css"/>
```

The first line of code is the CDN link for the Google Roboto font. The second line of code is for the Milligram CSS minified file.

Overview of the Milligram Framework

In this section, you will get an overview of the various attributes of Milligram before you learn how to build a product page with the framework.

- Milligram adheres to CSS3's *rem units* ideology for its typography wherein a single font size is defined for the root element and then all the other rem units are a percentage of that root, thereby providing easy maintainability and cleaner code. By the way, Milligram uses the Roboto font family as the default font for its typography.

- Block quotes in Milligram are quoted between the `<blockquote>` tags. A code element is defined between the `<code>` tags. If you are in need of a block, wrap the `<code>` element in the `<pre>` tags.

- The clearfix utility is used with the `clearfix` class, whereas a float is defined by the `float-left` and `float-right` classes depending on whether you want to float to the left and right, respectively.

- Similar to HTML, lists in Milligram are defined within the `<ol>`, `<ul>`, and `<dl>` tags for ordered, unordered, and description lists, respectively. Each list item is wrapped between the `<li>` tags similar to HTML.

- Buttons are defined by the `button` class with an anchor, `<a>`, tag. Alternatively, you can use the `<button>` element for defining the button. The default button is solid, whereas a bordered-only button without any solid color to it would need the `button-outline` class. For a clear button without borders or solid color, you can use the `button-clear` class.

- Tables in Milligram are similar to HTML tables where you use the `<thead>` and `<tbody>` elements. Similar to HTML, you use `<tr>` to define the table rows, `<td>` for the table data, and `<th>` for the table heading, and then you wrap everything within the main `<table>` element.

- Milligram, just like Skeleton, uses mobile-first queries that target the minimum width. Styles outside of a query apply to all devices. This is done to prevent small devices such as mobiles and tablets from parsing loads of unused CSS. Milligram uses the following media query sizes based on the device size:

- *Larger than mobile device/screen*: 40rem (640px)

- *Larger than tablet device/screen*: 80rem (1280px)

- *Larger than desktop device/screen*: 120rem (1920px)

Grid System in Milligram

Grids in Milligram use the CSS Flexible Box Layout module standard wherein the grid is fluid, shrinking based on the browser at smaller sizes. The entire grid system is responsive with a maximum width of 112rem (1120px).

See Listing 3-1 to understand the grid system in Milligram.

Listing 3-1. Grid System in Milligram

```
<!DOCTYPE html>
<html lang="en">
<head>
  <meta charset="utf-8">
  <title> Grid system</title>
  <meta name="description" content="">
  <meta name="author" content="">
  <meta name="viewport" content="width=device-width,
  initial-scale=1">

<link href="https://cdnjs.cloudflare.com/ajax/libs/milligram/
1.3.0/milligram.min.css" rel="stylesheet" type="text/css">
<link href="https://fonts.googleapis.com/css?family=Roboto"
rel="stylesheet">
</head>
<br>
```

```
<div class="container">
  <div class="row">
    <div style="text-align:center; border: 1px solid black;"
    class="column">One</div>
    <div style="text-align:center; border: 1px solid black;"
    class="column">Two</div>
    <div style="text-align:center; border: 1px solid black;"
    class="column">Three</div>
    <div style="text-align:center; border: 1px solid black;"
    class="column">Four</div>
  </div>
<br>
  <div class="row">
    <div style="text-align:center; border: 1px solid black;"
    class="column">One</div>
    <div style="text-align:center; border: 1px solid black;"
    class="column column-50 column-offset-25">Two</div>
  </div>
</div>
</html>
```

In the code, you use the CDN links for the Google fonts and the Milligram minified CSS file. You also define the viewport.

Just like Skeleton, the entire code is wrapped in a <div> element with a container class. All columns are defined within a row just like in many grid-based frameworks. However, Milligram is different from other frameworks in that you can add any number of columns within a row. You are not restricted to 12 columns like with many popular frameworks.

In Listing 3-1, initially you define a row within the <div> with the container class. Then, you define four columns within that row using the column class. You use inline styles for assigning a border and aligning the text to the center for each column.

Then you define another row and a column using a `column` class. Then you define another column within that row and use the `column-50` class along with the `column-offset-25` class. What the `column-50` class does is assign a column width of 50 percent to the column, which will allocate 50 percent of the column content within the parent row. The `column-offset-25` class moves the column to the right by 25 percent column space for that parent row.

Figure 3-4 shows the output of the code.

One	Two	Three	Four

One	Two

Figure 3-4. *Implementation of grid system of Milligram*

In Figure 3-4, you can see four columns, named One, Two, Three, and Four, in the first row. The second row has a column named One and a column named Two, which is offset by 25 percent and occupies 50 percent of the row width.

Building a Product Page with Milligram

Now that you have a brief idea about Milligram, you will learn how to create a product page with Milligram. The Product page contains information about a Virtual Private Network (VPN) along with its features and pricing.

Step 1: Defining the Header

Let's look at the code in Listing 3-2 to start the first step of building the secure VPN product page.

Listing 3-2. Defining the Header

```
<!DOCTYPE html>
<html>
    <head>
        <title>Secure VPN</title>
        <!--include milligram via cdn-->
        <meta name="viewport" content="width=device-width,
        initial-scale=1">
        <link href="https://cdnjs.cloudflare.com/ajax/libs/
        milligram/1.3.0/milligram.min.css" rel="stylesheet"
        type="text/css">
        <link href="https://fonts.googleapis.com/
        css?family=Roboto" rel="stylesheet">
        <link href="css/style.css" rel="stylesheet"
        type="text/css">
    </head>
    <body class="container">
        <div class="row contactArea">
            <!--Div with width of 50% and offset from left
            50%-->
            <div class="column column-50 column-offset-50">
                <div class="contactColumn">Your IP:
                115.166.129.152</div>
                <div class="contactColumn">Your Location:
                Unknown</div>
                <div class="contactColumn">Your Status:
                UNPROTECTED</div>
            </div>
        </div>
    </body>
</html>
```

In Listing 3-2, you define the viewport and add the CDN links for the fonts and the Milligram CSS minified file. Then you introduce a link for the `style.css` custom CSS file. After defining the links in the `<head>` tag, you create a `<body>` element with the container class in it. Then you define a `<div>` with the `row` class. You assign another custom class called `contactArea` to it, which you will use to define the custom CSS code.

Next, you define a `<div>` with a column of 50 percent width within the parent row and offset it by 50 percent within that row by using the `column-50` and `column-offset-50` classes. Within that `<div>`, you create three `<div>`s wherein you define the content that comprises the IP address, location, and status.

Then, you define the custom CSS code using the `contactArea` and `contactColumn` classes in the custom `style.css` file.

Listing 3-3 depicts the code in the `style.css` custom CSS file using the `contactArea` and `contactColumn` classes for the corresponding `<div>`s.

Listing 3-3. Defining CSS for the Header

```
.contactArea{
    background: #666;
    color: #fff;
    text-align: right
}
.contactColumn{
    font-size: 12px;
    display: inline-block;
    margin-right: 10px;
}
```

In Listing 3-3, you define the background as gray and the color of the words as white for the `contactArea` class. You align the text to the right.

For the `<div>` that is defined by the `contactArea` class, you define the font size as 12px and use a margin. You use the `display: inline-block` property, which essentially creates a grid of boxes that fills the browser width and wraps it. Here, it helps the content blocks of the header to retain their block-level characteristics and helps them appear next to each other without using a float attribute.

Figure 3-5 shows the output of the code.

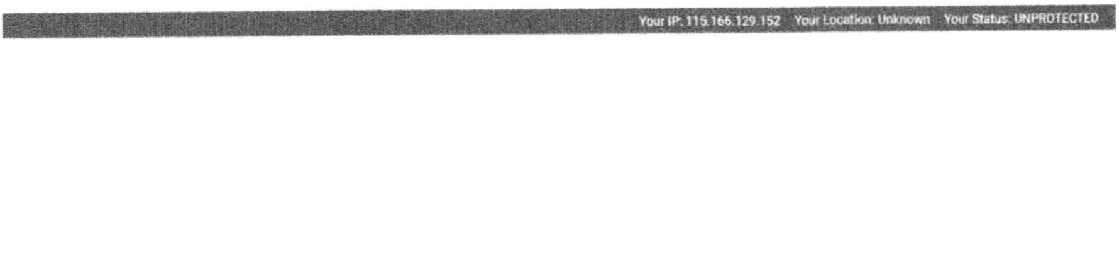

Your IP: 115.166.129.152   Your Location: Unknown   Your Status: UNPROTECTED

Figure 3-5. *Output of the header area*

In Figure 3-5, you can see the elements floated to the right with the IP address and the rest of the content.

Step 2: Defining the Navigation

Let's now look at the code in Listing 3-4 to proceed with step 2.

Listing 3-4. Defining the Navigation

```
<div class="navigation row">
    <div class="column column-25 logo">
        <img src="images/logo.png"/>
    </div>
    <div class="column column-50 column-offset-25">
        <a>Home</a>
        <a>Pricing</a>
        <a>Support</a>
        <a>Login</a>
    </div>
</div>
```

In Listing 3-4, you create a <div> and assign a row class to it. You also assign a custom navigation class to it, wherein you will define the custom CSS code in the style.css style sheet.

You then create a <div> within the <div> with the row class and assign a column width of 25 percent to it by using the column-25 class. You also add a logo custom class to it. You then insert an image for that <div> using the <img> element. The path to the images is set to the images folder, with the logo.png as the image name. Within the same row, you create another <div> and assign a column width of 50 percent to it using the column-50 class for that parent row, and you offset that column by 25 percent to the right.

You define the content in anchor link, <a>, tags.

Listing 3-5 shows the custom CSS code linked to the code in Listing 3-4.

Listing 3-5. Defining the CSS for the Navigation

```
.logo {
    text-align: left;
}
.logo img {
    width: 25%;
    margin: 10px 0;
}
.navigation{
    background: #ffc400;
    text-align: right;
    padding: 10px 0;
    font-weight: bold;
}
.navigation a{
    color: #000;
    padding: 5px;
    border: 2px solid #000;
}
```

As you can see in Listing 3-5, you define an image width of 25 percent and set a margin for it. In the navigation class, you define dark orange as the background color and align the text to the right. You set the padding and define the bold font weight for it. To the anchor links containing the Home, Pricing, Support, and Login links, you assign the black color and a black border with a padding of 5px. Figure 3-6 shows the output of the code.

In Figure 3-6, you can see the orange background and the links in the anchor tags (i.e., Home, Pricing, Support, and Login) to the right of the screen. You can also see the logo on the left of the screen.

Figure 3-6. *Output of the navigation*

Step 3: Defining the Banner Area

Let's look at the code in Listing 3-6 to see the next step in the coding process for the secure VPN product page.

Listing 3-6. HTML for the Banner Area

```
<section class="mastHead row">
        <div class="column column-60">
            <h2>Secure your data. Protect your privacy</h2>
            <h4>Protect your IP address and surf the web
            anonymously</h4>
        </div>
</section>
```

In Listing 3-6, you define the `<section>` tags and assign the row class as well as the custom `mastHead` class to it. Inside that row, you define a `<div>` with a column of 60 percent width for the row for the `<section>` tag.

Listing 3-7 shows the corresponding code for the `mastHead` class in the custom `style.css` style sheet.

Listing 3-7. CSS for the Banner Area

```
.mastHead {
    height: 450px;
    overflow: hidden;
    background: #ffc400;
    color: #000;
}
.mastHead h1,.mastHead h2,.mastHead h3,.mastHead h4,.mastHead
h5,.mastHead h6{
    color: #000
}
```

What you have done is set the height of the `<section>` with the `mastHead` class to 450px and set the background to dark orange, the same color as in step 2. Then, you define black color to the content in that section. You also set the color of all the headings in that section to black with the `mastHead` class.

Now you will split the sprite image shown in Figure 3-7 into three parts for the App Store, Google Play, and Windows Phone Store. The rest of the image for the Mac App Store and Windows PC will not be displayed on the page.

Figure 3-7. *Sprite image for store icons*

You define the code for the unordered list in Listing 3-8 within which you assign a column width of 60 percent, after the headings.

Listing 3-8. Adding Store Information to the Banner Area

```
<section class="mastHead row">
        <div class="column column-60">
            <h2>Secure your data. Protect your privacy</h2>
            <h4>Protect your IP address and surf the web
            anonymously</h4>
            <ul class="srote-badges">
                <li><a class="store-ios" title="Available
                on the App Store"></a></li>
```

```
                        <li><a class="store-android" title="Get it
                        on Google Play"></a></li>
                        <li><a class="store-winphone"
                        title="Download from Windows Phone
                        Store"></a></li>
                    </ul>
                </div>
</section>
```

As you can see from the code in Listing 3-8, you define the unordered list and assign the custom srote-badges class to it. You define the list in the anchor tags and assign the store-ios, store-android, and store-winphone custom classes to it.

The corresponding custom CSS code in the style.css style sheet for the unordered list will look like Listing 3-9.

Listing 3-9. Adding the CSS for Store Icons

```
ul.srote-badges{
    list-style: none;
}
ul.srote-badges li a, .srote-badges a {
    display: inline-block;
    background: url(../images/store-badges-70x245.png)
    no-repeat 0 0 #fff;
    width: 245px;
    height: 70px;
    border-radius: 4px;
}
.srote-badges a.store-ios {
    background-position: 0 0;
}
```

```
.srote-badges a.store-android {
    background-position: 0 -70px;
}
.srote-badges a.store-winphone {
    background-position: 0 -140px;
}
```

In Listing 3-9, you set list-style as none to remove the bullets. Further, you set the background as the sprite image by assigning the link to that image. Then, you define the width and height for it. You also assign a border-radius setting of 4px to the image. Next, you split the image into the first three parts and set the background position to 0 for the first part, -70px for the next part, and -140px for the third. The rest of the image cannot be seen.

Next you define an Android phone image, as shown in Figure 3-8, to the right using another <div> within the same section class.

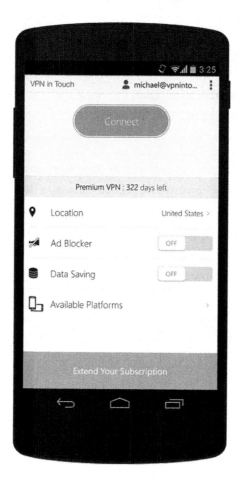

Figure 3-8. *Application image for the banner area*

You assign a column width of 40 percent for the parent <section> tag
and add the mastHeadImage class to it. Listing 3-10 shows the code within
the entire <section> tags after incorporating everything from the sprite
images into this Android image.

Listing 3-10. Adding the Application Image to the Banner Area

```
<section class="mastHead row">
        <div class="column column-60">
            <h2>Secure your data. Protect your privacy</h2>
            <h4>Protect your IP address and surf the web
            anonymously</h4>
            <ul class="srote-badges">
                <li><a class="store-ios" title="Available
                on the App Store"></a></li>
                <li><a class="store-android" title="Get it
                on Google Play"></a></li>
                <li><a class="store-winphone"
                title="Download from Windows Phone
                Store"></a></li>
            </ul>
        </div>
        <div class="column column-40 mastHeadImage"></div>
    </section>
```

Listing 3-11 shows the corresponding custom CSS code for the <div>
element with the last mastHeadImage class.

Listing 3-11. Adding the CSS for the Application Image in the
Banner Area

```
.mastHeadImage{
    background: url("../images/android-device1.png") no-repeat;
    background-size: cover;
    background-position: 0 15px;
}
```

In Listing 3-11, you refer to the background and assign the image link. Then you set `background-size` to `cover` and set `background-position` as 15px.

Figure 3-9 shows the output of the entire code so far.

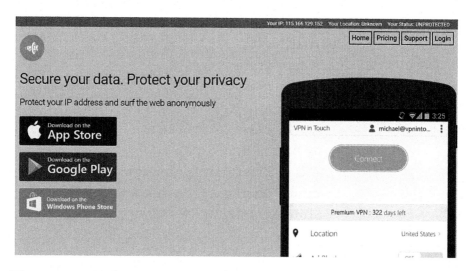

Figure 3-9. *Code output so far*

Step 4: Designing the Content Area

Moving Forward, you will design the content area.

Listing 3-12 shows how to proceed with building the "benefits" section.

Listing 3-12. HTML for the Content Area

```
<section class="info">
        <div class="row">
            <h3 class="column">BENEFITS OF USING VPN IN
            TOUCH</h3>
        </div>
```

```
<div class="row">
    <div class="column column-50">
        <h4>Unblock Websites</h4>
        <p>Bypass internet restriction and access
        to any websites: Unblock Facebook, Unblock
        Youtube.</p>
    </div>
    <div class="column column-50">
        <h4>Secure Your Data</h4>
        <p>Encrypt your private data before sending
        it from your computer, smartphone or tablet
        over the internet.</p>
    </div>
</div>
<div class="row">
    <div class="column column-50">
        <h4>Bypass content restrictions</h4>
        <p>Watch Netflix and BBC iPlayer, no matter
        where you are. Use Skype, Viber and all
        Voip services without restrictions.</p>
    </div>
    <div class="column column-50">
        <h4>Protect Your Privacy</h4>
        <p>Hide your IP address, protect your
        online identity while browsing and surf the
        web anonymously.</p>
    </div>
</div>
```

```
<div class="row">
    <div class="column column-50">
        <h4>Wifi Hotspot Security</h4>
        <p>Prevent sniffers and hackers from
        stealing your private data while using
        public hotspots.</p>
    </div>
    <div class="column column-50">
        <h4>Data Saving and Ad Blocker on Mobile</h4>
        <p>Save more bandwidth on your mobile 3G/4G
        data plan. Clear your mobile screen of
        obtrusive ads with Ad Blocking mode.</p>
    </div>
</div>
</section>
```

In Listing 3-12, you use a <section> tag and enclose a <div> with a row class. Within that parent row, you use the <h3> heading to define the content for the level 3 heading.

After that <div>, you create a <div> with the row class. You create two <div>s each with a column width of 50 percent of the parent <div> using the column-50 class. You define a level 4 <h4> and a paragraph element, <p>, with their respective content within each child <div>.

Repeat the process three more times, wherein you create two <div>s within a parent <div> with a row class. Similarly, define <h4> and <p> under each child <div> with their respective content.

Figure 3-10 shows the output of the code.

BENEFITS OF USING VPN IN TOUCH

Unblock Websites

Bypass internet restriction and access to any websites: Unblock Facebook, Unblock Youtube.

Bypass content restrictions

Watch Netflix and BBC iPlayer, no matter where you are. Use Skype, Viber and all Voip services without restrictions.

Wifi Hotspot Security

Prevent sniffers and hackers from stealing your private data while using public hotspots.

Secure Your Data

Encrypt your private data before sending it from your computer, smartphone or tablet over the internet.

Protect Your Privacy

Hide your IP address, protect your online identity while browsing and surf the web anonymously.

Data Saving and Ad Blocker on Mobile

Save more bandwidth on your mobile 3G/4G data plan. Clear your mobile screen of obtrusive ads with Ad Blocking mode.

Figure 3-10. *Output of the content area*

Step 5: Creating the Pricing Area

Next, you will create a pricing table wherein you will list the subscription price for the monthly, half-yearly, and yearly timeline.

Let's look at the code in Listing 3-13.

Listing 3-13. HTML for the Pricing Area

```
<section class="pricingInfo">
        <div class="row">
            <h3 class="column">Pricing Overview</h3>
        </div>
        <div class="row">
            <div  class="column">
            <table>
                <tbody>
                    <tr>
                        <td><strong>pricing</strong></td>
                        <td>1 Month</td>
                        <td>6 Months</td>
                        <td>1 Year</td>
                    </tr>
```

```
                        <tr>
                            <td><strong>Price</strong></td>
                            <td>$9.98/month</td>
                            <td>$2.99/month</td>
                            <td>$2.49/month</td>
                        </tr>
                        <tr>
                            <td><strong>Save</strong></td>
                            <td>0%</td>
                            <td>50%</td>
                            <td>75%</td>
                        </tr>
                    </tbody>
                </table>
                </div>
            </div>
        </section>
```

In Listing 3-13, you define the <section> tags within which you define the tables. Initially, you define a <div> with a row class where you use a heading of <h3> with the column class to define the content, i.e., Pricing Overview.

Then, you create a <div> with the row class after the preceding <div> and assign another <div> with the column class within it. Moving forward, you define the table headings and the table rows with the list of items in the table, which is quite similar to the way you create tables in HTML. Place the content within the <section> tags.

Figure 3-11 shows the output of the code.

Pricing Overview

pricing	1 Month	6 Months	1 Year
Price	$9.98/month	$2.99/month	$2.49/month
Save	0%	50%	75%

Figure 3-11. *Output of the pricing area*

Step 6: Creating the Footer

Finally, you will create a footer for your product page.

Let's look at the code in Listing 3-14 to understand how you design the footer of the web page.

Listing 3-14. HTML for the Footer

```
<footer>
          <div class="row">
              <div class="column column-25 logo">
                  <img src="images/logo.png"/>
                  <p>&copy; Copyright 2017</p>
                  <p>All rights reserved</p>
              </div>
              <div class="column column-25">
                  <h6>LEARN MORE</h6>
                  <a>Pricing</a><br>
                  <a>How To Setup</a><br>
                  <a>Servers</a><br>
                  <a>Blog</a><br>
                  <a>FAQ</a><br>
              </div>
              <div class="column column-25">
                  <h6>LEGAL</h6>
                  <a href="/legal#terms">Terms & Conditions
                  </a><br>
```

```
                    <a href="/legal#privacy">Privacy Policy
                    </a><br>
                    <a href="/legal#refund">Refund Policy
                    </a><br>
                </div>
            </div>
        </footer>
```

In Listing 3-14, you define the footer content within the `<footer>` tags. Inside the `<footer>` tags, you initially define a `<div>` with the row class. Then, you create three child `<div>`s each with a column with a width of 25 percent of the parent row so that each child `<div>` takes a quarter of the parent row space.

In the first child `<div>`, you assign a logo class to it. You then insert the logo image with the `<img>` tag. Then you enter the copyright information with the `<p>` tags.

For this first child `<div>`, you define the custom CSS code in the style.css file, as shown in Listing 3-15.

Listing 3-15. CSS for the Footer

```css
footer{
    color:#fff;
    background: #666;
    padding: 10px 0;
}
footer .logo img,footer .logo p{
    margin-left: 10px;
    display: block;
}
footer .logo p{
    margin-bottom: 0;
}
```

```
footer a{
    color: #fff;
}
footer h6{
    font-weight: bold;
    border-bottom: 1px solid #fff;
}
```

As you can see in Listing 3-15, you define the color, padding, and background for the `<footer>`. You define the left margin space and `display: block;` property for the footer and the image with the logo. Then, you assign the color to the anchors in the footer followed by defining the bold font and solid border for the footer and `<h6>` heading.

Back in Listing 3-14, you define the second child `<div>` and define the `<h6>` heading with the content, along with the links, which you define in the anchor tags.

The third child `<div>` contains the conditions and policy links defined between the `<h6>` and anchor `<a>` tags.

That sums up the code.

Figure 3-12 shows the snapshot of the footer part of the code.

Figure 3-12. *Output of the footer area*

Summary

In this chapter, you designed a page for a secure VPN product. Milligram is an awesome utility for lightweight projects. However, there are some constraints such as the maximum device size of 1120px and a lack of utility classes, which are required for massive immersive projects. Nevertheless, Milligram is an intuitive framework that doesn't come with the bulk of huge frameworks and is especially helpful when you want to build simple mobile web pages.

In the next chapter, you will look at another engaging framework, UIkit, which is quite useful for lightweight web projects.

CHAPTER 4

Introducing UIkit

UIkit, compared to Skeleton and Milligram, is quite expansive and comes with plenty of features that are handy for building interactive sites. It comes with bountiful HTML, CSS, and JavaScript components and can be easily customized to give a different feel to your web sites. Being lightweight and modular, its default styles help you build powerful interfaces adhering to the semantic protocols for web design.

It also comes with custom themes that can be downloaded from the Customizer section of the web site. A plethora of options help you get immersive web pages up and running in no time that work on all the modern browsers. In this chapter, we will shed light on the installation and grid concept before moving on to various features such as animations, icons, and accordions to help you get to grips with the flexibility that UIkit offers.

Installing UIkit

Go to the official web site at `https://getuikit.com/`. The Download button is on the upper-right side of the screen, as shown in Figure 4-1.

© Aravind Shenoy and Anirudh Prabhu 2018
A. Shenoy and A. Prabhu, *CSS Framework Alternatives*,
https://doi.org/10.1007/978-1-4842-3399-3_4

Figure 4-1. *UIkit download page*

After clicking Download, the zipped file gets downloaded. After unzipping the folder, the folder tree structure looks like Figure 4-2.

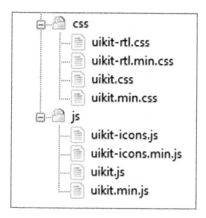

Figure 4-2. *Content of UIkit framework*

You can also install UIkit with prebuilt JavaScript, CSS, and Less source files with NPM, or you can clone the repo to get all the source files including build scripts.

To clone the repo, you need to use the following command:

```
git clone git://github.com/uikit/uikit.git
```

Another easy way to include the compiled files of all UIkit versions is to use the CDN files on the Cloudflare content delivery network. You include all the necessary files in your markup as shown in Listing 4-1.

Listing 4-1. Including UIkit in Your Web Page

```
<link rel="stylesheet" href="https://cdnjs.cloudflare.com/ajax/
libs/uikit/3.0.0-beta.28/css/uikit.min.css" />
<script src="https://cdnjs.cloudflare.com/ajax/libs/
jquery/3.2.1/jquery.min.js"></script>
<script src="https://cdnjs.cloudflare.com/ajax/libs/
uikit/3.0.0-beta.28/js/uikit.min.js"></script>
<script src="https://cdnjs.cloudflare.com/ajax/libs/
uikit/3.0.0-beta.28/js/uikit-icons.min.js"></script>
```

Grids, Cards, Flex, and Width

UIkit has a flexible grid system. UIkit's grid items are all stacked by default. To add a grid, you need to add the uk-grid attribute to the <div> element. Usually, we use the card component to demonstrate the grid functionality; the card element contains the card, the card body, and an optional card title.

Listing 4-2 depicts the code for the normal card component.

Listing 4-2. Card Component of UIkit

```
<html>
<head>
<!-- UIkit CSS -->
<link rel="stylesheet" href="https://cdnjs.cloudflare.com/ajax/
libs/uikit/3.0.0-beta.28/css/uikit.min.css" />
```

```
<!-- jQuery is required -->
<script src="https://cdnjs.cloudflare.com/ajax/libs/
jquery/3.2.1/jquery.min.js"></script>

<!-- UIkit JS -->
<script src="https://cdnjs.cloudflare.com/ajax/libs/
uikit/3.0.0-beta.28/js/uikit.min.js"></script>
<script src="https://cdnjs.cloudflare.com/ajax/libs/
uikit/3.0.0-beta.28/js/uikit-icons.min.js"></script>
</head>
<body style="padding:10px 10px 10px 10px;">
<div class="uk-card uk-card-default uk-card-body uk-width-1-2">
    <h3 class="uk-card-title">Cloud Computing</h3>
    <p>Cloud Computing is a computing infrastructure and
software model for enabling access to shared pools of
configurabel resources  such as computer networks, servers, and
storage including services which can be rapidly provisioned with
minimal management effort over the internet or intranet</p>
</div>
</body>
</html>
```

In this code, you include the links for the UIkit framework in the <head> section. You include the jQuery code, the UIkit JavaScript code, and the UIkit icon files in the links. Then, you create a <body> tag and assign a padding of 10px all over. Next, you create a <div> and assign the uk-card, uk-card-default, and uk-card-body classes in addition to assigning a width of half for the parent container using the uk-width-1-2 class. The uk-card class defines the card, while the uk-card-default class is the default styling for the card. The uk-card-body class defines the body for the card.

Then, you use the <h3> element to define a third-level heading for the card title and add a uk-card-title class to it. Next, you define random content within the <p> tags.

Figure 4-3 shows the output of the code.

Cloud Computing

Cloud Computing is a computing infrastructure and software model for enabling access to shared pools of configurabel resources such as computer networks, servers, and storage including services which can be rapidly provisioned with minimal managment effort over the internet or intranet

Figure 4-3. *Output of card component of UIkit*

You can have cards of different colors. Let's look at an example of how you assign different colors to the cards in UIkit; see Listing 4-3.

Listing 4-3. Adding Colors to the Card Component of UIkit

```
<div class="uk-child-width-1-3 uk-grid-small" uk-grid>
    <div>
        <div class="uk-card uk-card-default uk-card-body">
            <h3 class="uk-card-title">Default</h3>
            <p>Lorem ipsum dolor sit amet, consectetur
            adipisicing elit, sed do eiusmod tempor incididunt
            ut labore et dolore magna aliqua.</p>
        </div>
    </div>
    <div>
        <div class="uk-card uk-card-primary uk-card-body">
            <h3 class="uk-card-title">Primary color</h3>
            <p>Lorem ipsum dolor sit amet, consectetur
            adipisicing elit, sed do eiusmod tempor incididunt
            ut labore et dolore magna aliqua.</p>
        </div>
    </div>
    <div>
```

```
    <div class="uk-card uk-card-secondary uk-card-body">
        <h3 class="uk-card-title">Secondary</h3>
        <p>Lorem ipsum dolor sit amet, consectetur
        adipisicing elit, sed do eiusmod tempor incididunt
        ut labore et dolore magna aliqua.</p>
    </div>
  </div>
</div>
```

In the code sample in Listing 4-3, you create a parent `<div>` and assign a `uk-grid` attribute to it. By default, all items in the grid will be stacked. So, you assign a width class to the items to align it next to each other. In this example, to assign an equal width to all items within the parent `<div>`, you have to add a common `uk-child-width-1-3` class to it. What this class does is assign a width of one-third of the parent container to all the items in the grid. You also add a `uk-grid-small` class to it. This applies a small gutter. Usually, the grid component comes with a default gutter, but this `uk-grid-small` class applies a small gutter instead. Then, you create three child `<div>`s and assign the `uk-card` and `uk-card-default` and `uk-card-body` classes to create a normal card.

For the second item, you use a `uk-card-primary` class instead of the default class. For the third item, you use a `uk-card-secondary` class instead of the default class. You also assign the same title to all three items using the `uk-card-title` class within the `<h3>` tag for all three items.

Figure 4-4 shows the output of the code.

Figure 4-4. *Output of colored card components of UIkit*

Instead of the default styling, you can use a hover class so that you can create a hover effect on the card.

The only thing you need to do is add a uk-card-hover class to each child <div> for each of the items. The line will look as shown in Listing 4-4 where you use the uk-card-hover class for the <div> element with the default card color.

Listing 4-4. Adding Hover Effect to the Card Components

```
<div class="uk-card uk-card-default uk-card-hover uk-card-
body">
```

Similarly, you add the uk-card-hover class to the primary and secondary colored <div> items. On hovering, you can see the hover effect, which is quite handy in anchors and other aspects in web design.

You can use different size modifiers that will increase the padding in the card. Listing 4-5 contains the code that depicts how to use smaller and larger padding.

Listing 4-5. Using Size Modifiers with Card Components

```
<div class="uk-child-width-1-3@m uk-grid-small" uk-grid>
    <div>
        <div class="uk-card uk-card-default uk-card-small uk-
        card-hover uk-card-body">
            <h3 class="uk-card-title">Default</h3>
            <p>Lorem ipsum dolor sit amet, consectetur
            adipisicing elit, sed do eiusmod tempor incididunt
            ut labore et dolore magna aliqua.</p>
        </div>
    </div>
    <div>
```

```
<div class="uk-card uk-card-primary uk-card-large
uk-card-hover uk-card-body">
    <h3 class="uk-card-title">Primary color</h3>
    <p>Lorem ipsum dolor sit amet, consectetur
    adipisicing elit, sed do eiusmod tempor incididunt
    ut labore et dolore magna aliqua.</p>
    </div>
    </div>
    <div>

    </div>
</div>
```

Here you define two cards with the same content, but you use uk-card-small for the child <div> for the default card and use the uk-card-large class for the child <div> with the primary color.

The rest of the code is the same for both child <div>s.

Figure 4-5 shows the output of the code.

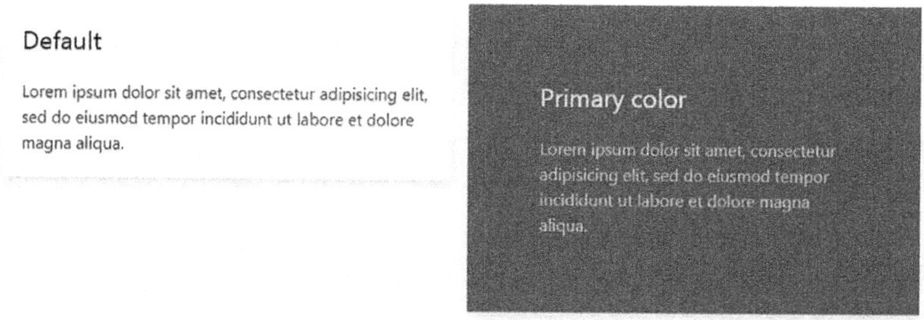

Figure 4-5. *Output of using size modifier with card component*

The width class is used in conjunction with the card component to split content into responsive columns. Now let's understand the width class better using some examples; see Listing 4-6.

Listing 4-6. Using Width Classes Along with Card Component

```
<div class="uk-text-center" uk-grid>
    <div class="uk-width-1-3">
        <div class="uk-card uk-card-primary uk-card-default
        uk-card-body">One Third</div>
    </div>
    <div class="uk-width-1-3">
        <div class="uk-card uk-card-primary uk-card-default
        uk-card-body">One Third</div>
    </div>
    <div class="uk-width-1-3">
        <div class="uk-card uk-card-primary uk-card-default
        uk-card-body">One Third</div>
    </div>
</div>

<div class="uk-text-center" uk-grid>
    <div class="uk-width-1-2">
        <div class="uk-card uk-card-default uk-card-
        body">Half</div>
    </div>
    <div class="uk-width-1-2">
        <div class="uk-card uk-card-default uk-card-
        body">Half</div>
    </div>
</div>
<div class="uk-text-center" uk-grid>
    <div class="uk-width-1-4">
        <div class="uk-card uk-card-default uk-card-secondary
        uk-card-body">One-fourth</div>
    </div>
```

```
<div class="uk-width-3-4">
    <div class="uk-card uk-card-default uk-card-secondary
    uk-card-body">Three-fourth</div>
</div>
</div>
```

In the preceding code sample, you create a parent <div> under which you center the text for all the items by using a uk-text-center class in the parent <div>. Then, you add a uk-grid attribute for the parent <div>.

For each child <div>, you use a width of one-third for each item in the parent container (i.e., the parent <div>). You define the code for the card in a <div> within the <div> for each item containing the width class.

Similarly, you create another parent <div>. Here you use the same coding strategy, but you use two child items. You assign a width of half for each item for that parent <div>. Also in the previous parent <div>, you use a primary color for all the items. Here you use the default color for the cards.

You move on to create another parent <div> with the uk-grid attribute like in the previous parent <div>s. Here you create two <div>s, but you assign a secondary color to the cards, and you assign a width of one-quarter to the first item and three-quarters to the second item using the uk-width-1-4 and uk-width-3-4 classes.

Figure 4-6 shows the output of the code.

Figure 4-6. *Output of the code so far*

Instead of assigning a width to each item, if the items are of the same size, then you can use the uk-child-width-* class to it where * stands for the dimensions of each items. For example, uk-child-width-1-4 will apply a width of one-quarter of the parent container to all the items.

Let's look at this with a code sample; see Listing 4-7.

Listing 4-7. Using the uk-child-width-* Class to Adjust the Width of the Inner Components

```
<div class="uk-child-width-1-4 uk-grid-small uk-text-center"
uk-grid>
    <div>
        <div class="uk-card uk-card-default uk-card-primary uk-
        card-body">Cloud</div>
    </div>
    <div>
        <div class="uk-card uk-card-default uk-card-primary uk-
        card-body">Cloud</div>
    </div>
    <div>
        <div class="uk-card uk-card-default uk-card-primary uk-
        card-body">Cloud</div>
    </div>
    <div>
        <div class="uk-card uk-card-default uk-card-primary uk-
        card-body">Cloud</div>
    </div>
    <div>
        <div class="uk-card uk-card-default uk-card-primary uk-
        card-body">Cloud</div>
    </div>
</div>
```

79

In the code, you use a common uk-child-width-1-4 in all items in the parent <div>. Then you define the child <div>s with the card element code.

Figure 4-7 shows the output of the code.

Figure 4-7. *Using the uk-child-width-* class to adjust the width of the inner components*

As you can see in Figure 4-7, the width classes with fractions will break in to a new row if they exceed their container's width. However, to evenly split them in the same row, you can use the expand class as shown in Listing 4-8.

Listing 4-8. Implementing uk-child-width-expand for Evenly Sizing the Inner Elements

```
<div class="uk-child-width-expand uk-grid-small uk-text-center"
uk-grid>
    <div>
        <div class="uk-card uk-card-default uk-card-primary uk-
        card-body">Cloud</div>
    </div>
    <div>
        <div class="uk-card uk-card-default uk-card-primary uk-
        card-body">Cloud</div>
    </div>
    <div>
        <div class="uk-card uk-card-default uk-card-primary uk-
        card-body">Cloud</div>
    </div>
```

```
<div>
    <div class="uk-card uk-card-default uk-card-primary uk-
    card-body">Cloud</div>
</div>
<div>
    <div class="uk-card uk-card-default uk-card-primary uk-
    card-body">Cloud</div>
</div>
</div>
```

As you can see, you can use uk-child-width-expand to evenly split all the items in the same row without going to the next row. Figure 4-8 shows the output of the code.

Figure 4-8. *Evenly sizing the inner elements*

You can also define a custom width for some items in the code and use them in conjunction with the uk-child-width classes. Let's look at the code in Listing 4-9 to see an example.

Listing 4-9. Defining Custom Width for Inner Element

```
<div class="uk-child-width-expand uk-grid-small uk-text-center"
uk-grid>
    <div>
        <div class="uk-card uk-card-default uk-card-primary uk-
        card-body"> Spread</div>
    </div>
    <div class="uk-width-2-3">
        <div class="uk-card uk-card-default uk-card-primary uk-
        card-body">Custom </div>
    </div>
```

81

```
<div>
    <div class="uk-card uk-card-default uk-card-primary uk-
    card-body">Spread</div>
</div>
<div>
    <div class="uk-card uk-card-default uk-card-primary
    uk-card-body">Spread</div>
</div>
</div>
```

In Listing 4-9, you use uk-child-width-expand as the common class to the parent <div>. However, in the second child <div>, you use a custom width of uk-width-2-3 and let the other child <div>s remain the same. What happens is that the second item will encompass a width of two-thirds the parent container, while the other items will be evenly split in the same row.

Figure 4-9 shows the output of the code.

Figure 4-9. *Defining custom width for inner elements*

You can use the FlexBox component in UIkit. It helps you build interactive grid layouts. Let's look at an example to understand it better; Listing 4-10 shows an example of how FlexBox can be used.

Listing 4-10. Using FlexBox with UIkit

```
<div class="uk-flex">
    <div class="uk-card uk-card-default uk-card-primary uk-
    card-body">First</div>
    <div class="uk-card uk-card-default uk-card-primary uk-
    card-body uk-margin-left">Second</div>
```

```
<div class="uk-card uk-card-default uk-card-primary uk-
    card-body uk-margin-left">Third</div>
</div>
```

In the code, you use the uk-flex class with the parent <div>. Then, you define three items in the child <div>s and use a uk-margin-left for the second and third items to create space between the items. By default, all items will be aligned to the left along with the content and height, as shown in Figure 4-10.

Figure 4-10. *Using FlexBox with UIkit*

You can align the flex items to the right and center and even add equal space between the items using the uk-flex-right, uk-flex-center, and uk-flex-around classes.

Listing 4-11 shows the code where all the items are centered.

Listing 4-11. Aligning Flex Item

```
<div class="uk-flex uk-flex-center">
    <div class="uk-card uk-card-default uk-card-primary
    uk-card-body">First</div>
    <div class="uk-card uk-card-default uk-card-primary
    uk-card-body uk-margin-left">Second</div>
    <div class="uk-card uk-card-default uk-card-primary
    uk-card-body uk-margin-left">Third</div>
</div>
```

Figure 4-11 shows the output of the code.

Figure 4-11. *Aligning flex items*

You can use responsive classes with the flex items where @s added to the flex classes will affect device widths of 640px or higher, @m affects device widths of 960px or higher, @l affects device widths of 1200px or higher, and @xl affects device widths of 1600px or higher. See Listing 4-12.

Listing 4-12. Using Responsive Classes with Flex Items

```
<div class="uk-flex uk-flex-left@m uk-flex-center@l">
    <div class="uk-card uk-card-default uk-card-primary uk-
    card-body">FIRST</div>
    <div class="uk-card uk-card-default uk-card-primary uk-
    card-body uk-margin-left">SECOND</div>
    <div class="uk-card uk-card-default uk-card-primary uk-
    card-body uk-margin-left">THIRD</div>
</div>
```

In the code in Listing 4-12, you define uk-flex-left@m and uk-flex-center@l to the parent <div>s.

Then you define the child <div>s just like in the previous examples. On the large screen, the flex items will be centered, whereas the items will be aligned to the left on a small screen.

The vertical alignment of items is possible in Flexbox. Let's look at an example in Listing 4-13. You can also define the item order as shown in the same example.

Listing 4-13. Vertically Aligning the Flex Items

```
<div class="uk-flex uk-flex-column uk-text-center uk-
width-1-3">
    <div class="uk-card uk-card-default uk-card-primary uk-card-body
    uk-flex-last@m uk-flex-first@l uk-margin-top">Cloud 1</div>
    <div class="uk-card uk-card-default uk-card-primary uk-card-
    body uk-margin-top">Cloud 2</div>
    <div class="uk-card uk-card-default uk-card-primary uk-card-body
    uk-flex-first@m uk-flex-last@l uk-margin-top">Cloud 3</div>
</div>
```

As you can see, you can use uk-flex-column in the parent <div>. So, the output will be as shown in Figure 4-12.

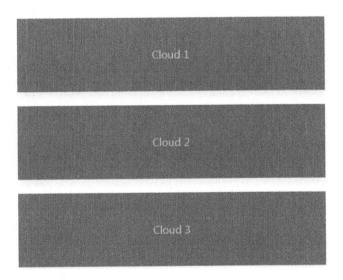

Figure 4-12. *Vertically aligning the flex items*

85

However, in the same code in Listing 4-13, you define responsive classes in the first and third items. You use `uk-flex-last@m` and `uk-flex-first@l` for the first item. You use `uk-flex-first@m uk-flex-last@l` for the third item. Therefore, while the preceding output was for the large screen, on small and medium screens, the first item, Cloud 1, will be the last item, whereas the third item, Cloud 3, will be the first item, as shown in Figure 4-13.

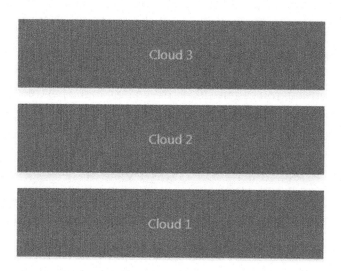

Figure 4-13. *Vertically aligning the flex item*

Finally, coming back to grids, you can also use nested grids in UIkit. Let's look at the code in Listing 4-14 to understand it better.

Listing 4-14. Using Nested Grids in UIkit

```
<div class="uk-child-width-1-2 uk-text-center" uk-grid>
    <div>
        <div class="uk-card uk-card-default uk-card-primary uk-
        card-body">FIrst 1-1</div>
    </div>
```

```
<div>
    <div class="uk-child-width-1-2 uk-text-center" uk-grid>
        <div>
            <div class="uk-card uk-card-primary uk-card-
            body">Nested 2-1 </div>
        </div>
        <div>
            <div class="uk-card uk-card-primary uk-card-
            body">Nested 2-2</div>
        </div>
    </div>
</div>
</div>
```

Here, you create a parent <div> and assign a child width of half to it. Then, you create two child <div>s. You define a normal card in the first child <div>. However, in the second child <div>, you assign a width of half for each subchild <div>.

Figure 4-14 shows the output of the code.

Figure 4-14. *Using nested grid in UIkit*

You can match the height of all the <div>s irrespective of the content of all the items. Listing 4-15 shows the code for this.

Listing 4-15. Matching the Heights of the Elements

```
<div class="uk-grid-match uk-child-width-expand@s uk-text-
center" uk-grid>
    <div>
        <div class="uk-card uk-card-primary uk-card-body">Lorem
        ipsum dolor sit amet, consectetur adipisicing elit</div>
    </div>
    <div>
        <div class="uk-card uk-card-primary uk-card-body">Lorem
        ipsum dolor sit amet, consectetur adipisicing elitLorem
        ipsum dolor sit amet, consectetur adipisicing elit</div>
    </div>
    <div>
        <div class="uk-card uk-card-primary uk-card-body">Lorem
        ipsum dolor sit amet, consectetur adipisicing elitLorem
        ipsum dolor sit amet, consectetur adipisicing elitLorem
        ipsum dolor sit amet, consectetur adipisicing elitLorem
        ipsum dolor sit amet, consectetur adipisicing elit</
        div>
    </div>
</div>
```

As you can see, you use the uk-grid-match class in the parent <div>.
Then, you create three items just as in the previous examples.

Figure 4-15 shows the output of the code.

Figure 4-15. *Output of the code so far*

Animations

UIkit has a plethora of animations that impart a certain degree of immersive behavior to your web sites. Let's look at the example in Listing 4-16 to understand the behavior of animations in a web page.

Listing 4-16. Adding Animation

```
<div class="uk-child-width-1-4 uk-grid-match" uk-grid>
    <div class="uk-animation-toggle">
        <div class="uk-card uk-card-primary uk-card-body
        uk-animation-fade">
            <p class="uk-text-center">Fade</p>
        </div>
    </div>
    <div class="uk-animation-toggle">
        <div class="uk-card uk-card-primary uk-card-body
        uk-animation-scale-up">
            <p class="uk-text-center">Scale Up</p>
        </div>
    </div>
    <div class="uk-animation-toggle">
        <div class="uk-card uk-card-primary uk-card-body
        uk-animation-scale-down">
            <p class="uk-text-center">Scale Down</p>
        </div>
    </div>
    <div class="uk-animation-toggle">
        <div class="uk-card uk-card-primary uk-card-body
        uk-animation-shake">
            <p class="uk-text-center">Shake</p>
        </div>
```

```
        </div>
        <div class="uk-animation-toggle">
            <div class="uk-card uk-card-primary uk-card-body uk-
            animation-slide-left">
                <p class="uk-text-center">Left</p>
            </div>
        </div>
        <div class="uk-animation-toggle">
            <div class="uk-card uk-card-primary uk-card-body uk-
            animation-slide-top">
                <p class="uk-text-center">Top</p>
            </div>
        </div>
        <div class="uk-animation-toggle">
            <div class="uk-card uk-card-primary uk-card-body uk-
            animation-slide-bottom">
                <p class="uk-text-center">Bottom</p>
            </div>
        </div>
        <div class="uk-animation-toggle">
            <div class="uk-card uk-card-primary uk-card-body uk-
            animation-slide-right">
                <p class="uk-text-center">Right</p>
            </div>
        </div>
    </div>
</div>
```

In Listing 4-16, you create the parent `<div>` to which you assign the
`uk-child-width-1-4` class. This aligns the items in a row with each item
taking one-quarter of the space of the parent container. You assign the
`uk-grid` attribute as in the previous examples. Then, you proceed to create
eight child `<div>`s. To each child `<div>`, you assign the `uk-animation-toggle`

class due to which there will be a hover effect that will trigger the animation. Then, you create a card in a sub `<div>` inside those child `<div>`s.

Since there are eight items, you assign these eight animation classes to each child `<div>`:

- `uk-animation-fade` class for the first child `<div>`

  This creates a fade effect for the item.

- `uk-animation-scale-up` class for the second child `<div>`

  This creates a fade effect wherein the item scales up.

- `uk-animation-scale-down` for the third child `<div>`

  This creates a fade effect where the item scales down.

- `uk-animation-shake` for the fourth child `<div>`

  This creates a shake effect wherein the item seems to vibrate.

- `uk-animation-slide-left` for the fifth `<div>`

  The item slides from the left.

- `uk-animation-slide-top` for the sixth `<div>`

  The item slides from the top.

- `uk-animation-slide-bottom` for the seventh `<div>`

  The item slides from the bottom.

- `uk-animation-slide-right` for the eight `<div>`

  This item slides from the right.

Figure 4-16 shows the output of the code.

Figure 4-16. *Adding animation*

When you hover over the items, you can see the animation effect as defined in the code. For example, when you hover over the first item, it will fade. On hovering over the fifth item, the item will slide from the left.

You can also define the space or distance of the animation. All you need to do is add the appropriate top, right, bottom, or left animation class.

For example, `uk-animation-slide-left-small` will create a left sliding effect from a shorter distance, whereas `uk-animation-slide-left-medium` will create a left sliding effect from a longer distance. The distance is already predefined by a fixed pixel value.

Let's look at the code example in Listing 4-17 to understand it better.

Listing 4-17. Adding Animations with Space and Distance

```
<div class=" uk-child-width-1-4 uk-grid-match" uk-grid>
   <div class="uk-animation-toggle">
       <div class="uk-card uk-card-primary uk-card-body uk-
       animation-slide-left-small">
           <p class="uk-text-center">Left Small</p>
       </div>
   </div>
   <div class="uk-animation-toggle">
       <div class="uk-card uk-card-primary uk-card-body uk-
       animation-slide-top-small">
           <p class="uk-text-center">Top Small</p>
       </div>
   </div>
```

```
<div class="uk-animation-toggle">
    <div class="uk-card uk-card-primary uk-card-body uk-
    animation-slide-bottom-small">
        <p class="uk-text-center">Bottom Small</p>
    </div>
</div>
<div class="uk-animation-toggle">
    <div class="uk-card uk-card-primary uk-card-body uk-
    animation-slide-right-small">
        <p class="uk-text-center">Right Small</p>
    </div>
</div>
<div class="uk-animation-toggle">
    <div class="uk-card uk-card-primary uk-card-body uk-
    animation-slide-left-medium">
        <p class="uk-text-center">Left Medium</p>
    </div>
</div>
<div class="uk-animation-toggle">
    <div class="uk-card uk-card-primary uk-card-body uk-
    animation-slide-top-medium">
        <p class="uk-text-center">Top Medium</p>
    </div>
</div>
<div class="uk-animation-toggle">
    <div class="uk-card uk-card-primary uk-card-body uk-
    animation-slide-bottom-medium">
        <p class="uk-text-center">Bottom Medium</p>
    </div>
</div>
```

```
<div class="uk-animation-toggle">
    <div class="uk-card uk-card-primary uk-card-body uk-
    animation-slide-right-medium">
        <p class="uk-text-center">Right Medium</p>
    </div>
</div>
</div>
```

In Listing 4-17, you follow the same code as in Listing 4-16, the only difference being the addition of the distance to the animation class. You define the classes as uk-animation-slide-left-small, uk-animation-slide-top-small, uk-animation-slide-bottom-small, and uk-animation-slide-right-small to create the sliding animation effect from the left, top, bottom, and right for a shorter distance. Similarly, you use the uk-animation-slide-left-medium, uk-animation-slide-top-medium, uk-animation-slide-bottom-medium, and uk-animation-slide-right-medium classes to define a medium distance for the sliding effect animation from the left, top, bottom, and right.

Figure 4-17 shows the output of the code.

Figure 4-17. *Adding animations with space and distance*

When you hover over the items, they will display the behavior as defined and explained in the code. For example, when you hover over the sixth item, the item will slide in from the top from a larger distance compared to the second item, which slides from the top in a shorter distance.

If you observe the animations so far, all of them are incoming; however, to make them outgoing, you can use the reverse function. All you need to do is add a uk-animation-reverse class to the element, as shown in Listing 4-18.

Listing 4-18. Adding Reverse Animation

```
<div class="uk-child-width-1-2 uk-grid-match" uk-grid>
    <div class="uk-animation-toggle">
        <div class="uk-card uk-card-primary uk-card-body uk-
        animation-fade uk-animation-reverse">
            <p class="uk-text-center">Fade</p>
        </div>
    </div>

    <div class="uk-animation-toggle">
        <div class="uk-card uk-card-primary uk-card-body uk-
        animation-slide-right uk-animation-reverse">
            <p class="uk-text-center">Right</p>
        </div>
    </div>
</div>
```

In Listing 4-18, you create two card items inside the parent <div> that span half of the parent grid. For the first child <div>, you define the fade animation class followed by the uk-animation-reverse class. For the second child <div>, you define the animation sliding effect from the right. However, you also define the uk-animation-reverse class to it similar to the first child <div>.

Figure 4-18 shows the output of the code.

Figure 4-18. *Adding reverse animation*

When you click the first item, it will fade in the reverse way (i.e., outgoing). Similarly, when you click the second item, it will slide from left to the right (i.e., in the reverse direction) and fade away.

Scrollspy with Animations

Scrollspy helps you trigger events when you scroll your page. It can be used with the animation class extensively to create an awesome effect for your web pages.

Let's understand it by means of a coding example, as shown in Listing 4-19. (Inside the <p> tags, there is a load of content. For the entire content, refer to the code bundle.)

Listing 4-19. Adding Scrollspy

```
<body style="padding:10px 10px 10px 10px;">
<p>
Lorem ipsum ....(loads of text)
</p>
<p>
Lorem ipsum ....(loads of text)
</p>
<div class="uk-child-width-1-2@m uk-grid-match" uk-grid>
    <div>
        <div class="uk-card uk-card-primary uk-card-body" uk-
        scrollspy="cls: uk-animation-slide-left; repeat: true">
            <h3 class="uk-card-title">Cloud</h3>
            <p>Cloud Computing is the new revolution</p>
        </div>
    </div>
    <div>
```

```
    <div class="uk-card uk-card-primary uk-card-body"
    uk-scrollspy="cls: uk-animation-slide-right; repeat:
    true">
        <h3 class="uk-card-title">Cloud</h3>
        <p>Cloud Computing is the new revolution</p>
    </div>
    </div>
</div>
</body>
```

In Listing 4-19, you define two paragraph elements and fill them with loads of text. Then you define a <div> class, and to this parent <div> you assign a uk-child-width-1-2@m class to define the width of the two child <div> elements within the grid defined by the uk-grid-match and uk-grid classes. Then you create two child <div>s; you create basically two card items, and you assign the uk-scrollspy="cls: uk-animation-slide-left; repeat: true" attribute to the first child <div> and uk-scrollspy="cls: uk-animation-slide-right; repeat: true" to the second child <div>. This will make the cards slide from the left and right, respectively, when you scroll down to that section of the page. You use the repeat: true property to repeat the effects when you scroll to that section of the page.

The output of the code will display two paragraphs of content. When you scroll down the page, the cards will slide from the left and right automatically. Figure 4-19 displays the two cards, which slide in from the left and right, respectively, when you scroll to that section.

orci consectetur interdum. Nunc id lacus neque. Maecenas porttitor ligula sed lectus facilisis, non auctor mauris eleifend. Vivamus blandit a nibh iaculis iaculis. Vivamus faucibus tincidunt enim id vulputate. Donec quis posuere erat, sit amet ullamcorper lacus. Aenean neque odio, bibendum non dictum commodo, viverra sed risus. Proin hendrerit orci at pellentesque lobortis. Mauris egestas dolor ante, a posuere mauris scelerisque quis. Curabitur nunc arcu, cursus nec diam nec, porttitor lacinia sem. Pellentesque iaculis, ligula ut pulvinar consectetur, ante nibh aliquam lectus, ut facilisis dui magna ut urna.Lorem ipsum dolor sit amet, consectetur adipiscing elit. Sed lectus risus, iaculis et odio vel, consequat porttitor tortor. Pellentesque magna est, tincidunt vel porta quis, sagittis vel lectus. Mauris sed lobortis velit, id scelerisque enim. Phasellus et turpis eu orci consectetur interdum. Nunc id lacus neque. Maecenas porttitor ligula sed lectus facilisis, non auctor mauris eleifend. Vivamus blandit a nibh iaculis iaculis. Vivamus faucibus tincidunt enim id vulputate. Donec quis posuere erat, sit amet ullamcorper lacus. Aenean neque odio, bibendum non dictum commodo, viverra sed risus. Proin hendrerit orci at pellentesque lobortis. Mauris egestas dolor ante, a posuere mauris scelerisque quis. Curabitur nunc arcu, cursus nec diam nec, porttitor lacinia sem. Pellentesque iaculis, ligula ut pulvinar consectetur, ante nibh aliquam lectus, ut facilisis dui magna ut urna.

Figure 4-19. *Adding Scrollspy*

If you want to create items with the same animation effect, you do not have to define the Scrollspy animation separately for each item. You can club them together by using the target property to the class in the scrollspy attribute. Listing 4-20 shows an example of this.

Listing 4-20. Adding Scrollspy

```
<p>..
Lorem Ipsum...(loads of text)...
</p>
<p>
Lorem ipsum (loads of text)...
</p>

<div class="uk-child-width-1-3@m" uk-grid uk-scrollspy="cls:
uk-animation-slide-top; target: > div > .uk-card; delay: 500;
repeat: true">
    <div>
        <div class="uk-card uk-card-primary uk-card-body">
            <h3 class="uk-card-title">Top Animation</h3>
            <p>Animation effect: Slides from the Top</p>
        </div>
    </div>
```

```
<div>
    <div class="uk-card uk-card-primary uk-card-body">
        <h3 class="uk-card-title">Top Animation</h3>
        <p>Animation effect: Slides from the Top</p>
    </div>
</div>
<div>
    <div class="uk-card uk-card-primary uk-card-body">
        <h3 class="uk-card-title">Top Animation</h3>
        <p>Animation effect: Slides from the Top</p>
    </div>
</div>
</div>
```

In Listing 4-20, you define the grid and assign the uk-child-width-1-3@m class to it to assign a width of one-third of the parent container width. Then, you apply the following scroll spy property to the parent <div>:

uk-scrollspy="cls: uk-animation-slide-top; target: > div > .uk-card; delay: 500; repeat: true"

This defines the animation for all the child items when you scroll down to that section. Here, you use cls: uk-animation-slide-top to create an animation effect wherein the element slides from the top. Then, you follow it up with target: > div > .uk-card; in the same line, which will target the card defined by the <div> with the uk-card class. Thereon, you create a delay of 500ms and use the repeat attribute here too. Next, you go on to create three card items.

The output of the code will show text, and on scrolling down below the text, the three card items will slide in from the top, as shown in Figure 4-20.

orci consectetur interdum. Nunc id lacus neque. Maecenas porttitor ligula sed lectus facilisis, non auctor mauris eleifend. Vivamus blandit a nibh iaculis iaculis. Vivamus faucibus tincidunt enim id vulputate. Donec quis posuere erat, sit amet ullamcorper lacus. Aenean neque odio, bibendum non dictum commodo, viverra sed risus. Proin hendrerit orci at pellentesque lobortis. Mauris egestas dolor ante, a posuere mauris scelerisque quis. Curabitur nunc arcu, cursus nec diam nec, porttitor lacinia sem. Pellentesque iaculis, ligula ut pulvinar consectetur, ante nibh aliquam lectus, ut facilisis dui magna ut urna.Lorem ipsum dolor sit amet, consectetur adipiscing elit. Sed lectus risus, iaculis et odio vel, consequat porttitor tortor. Pellentesque magna est, tincidunt vel porta quis, sagittis vel lectus. Mauris sed lobortis velit, id scelerisque enim. Phasellus et turpis eu orci consectetur interdum. Nunc id lacus neque. Maecenas porttitor ligula sed lectus facilisis, non auctor mauris eleifend. Vivamus blandit a nibh iaculis iaculis. Vivamus faucibus tincidunt enim id vulputate. Donec quis posuere erat, sit amet ullamcorper lacus. Aenean neque odio, bibendum non dictum commodo, viverra sed risus. Proin hendrerit orci at pellentesque lobortis. Mauris egestas dolor ante, a posuere mauris scelerisque quis. Curabitur nunc arcu, cursus nec diam nec, porttitor lacinia sem. Pellentesque iaculis, ligula ut pulvinar consectetur, ante nibh aliquam lectus, ut facilisis dui magna ut urna.

Figure 4-20. *Adding Scrollspy*

Accordions

An accordion helps to stack items, which, when clicked, will display information. It helps reduce the overload of information on a web page.

Listing 4-21 shows an example of an accordion in UIkit.

Listing 4-21. Adding an Accordion

```
<ul uk-accordion>
    <li class="uk-open">
        <h3 class="uk-accordion-title"> Cloud</h3>
        <div class="uk-accordion-content">
            <p>Lorem ipsum dolor sit amet, consectetur
            adipiscing elit. Nam fermentum justo urna. Nam
            blandit diam ac erat congue, ullamcorper vulputate
            odio tempus. Quisque maximus dolor sit amet nisi
            lacinia euismod. Pellentesque laoreet, tortor
            malesuada volutpat luctus, augue diam venenatis
            risus</p>
        </div>
    </li>
    <li>
        <h3 class="uk-accordion-title"> Cloud</h3>
        <div class="uk-accordion-content">
```

```
        <p>Lorem ipsum dolor sit amet, consectetur
        adipiscing elit. Nam fermentum justo urna. Nam
        blandit diam ac erat congue, ullamcorper vulputate
        odio tempus. Quisque maximus dolor sit amet nisi
        lacinia euismod. Pellentesque laoreet, tortor
        malesuada volutpat luctus, augue diam venenatis
        risus</p>
      </div>
    </li>
    <li>
      <h3 class="uk-accordion-title"> Cloud</h3>
      <div class="uk-accordion-content">
        <p>Lorem ipsum dolor sit amet, consectetur
        adipiscing elit. Nam fermentum justo urna. Nam
        blandit diam ac erat congue, ullamcorper vulputate
        odio tempus. Quisque maximus dolor sit amet nisi
        lacinia euismod. Pellentesque laoreet, tortor
        malesuada volutpat luctus, augue diam venenatis
        risus</p>
      </div>
    </li>
</ul>
```

In Listing 4-21, you create a list using the <ul> tag. You need to assign the uk-accordion class to it. This will create the accordion. Then, you create three list items using the <li> tags.

You assign the uk-open class to the first list item so that it is open by default. Inside the first item, you define the heading of the accordion using the uk-accordion-title class with the <h3> tag. Then, you create a <div> and assign the uk-accordion-content class to it. You define the content within that <div> using the paragraph <p> tags; similarly, to the other two list items, you define the content and heading of the accordion. However, remember not to use the uk-open class for these two list items as the uk-open class is to be used only for that accordion that displays content by default.

Figure 4-21 shows the output of the code.

Cloud   −

Lorem ipsum dolor sit amet, consectetur adipiscing elit. Nam fermentum justo urna. Nam blandit diam ac erat congue, ullamcorper vulputate odio tempus. Quisque maximus dolor sit amet nisi lacinia euismod. Pellentesque laoreet, tortor malesuada volutpat luctus, augue diam venenatis risus

Cloud   +

Cloud   +

Figure 4-21. *Adding an accordion*

If you want all the accordions to show the content without the other collapsing, then use the multiple: true property with the uk-accordion attribute. Listing 4-22 shows an example of multiple accordions that are open and shows content without collapsing.

Listing 4-22. Adding Multiple Accordions

```
<ul uk-accordion="multiple: true">
    <li class="uk-open">
        <h3 class="uk-accordion-title"> Cloud</h3>
        <div class="uk-accordion-content">
            <p>Lorem ipsum dolor sit amet, consectetur
            adipiscing elit. Nam fermentum justo urna. Nam
            blandit diam ac erat congue, ullamcorper vulputate
            odio tempus. Quisque maximus dolor sit amet nisi
            lacinia euismod. Pellentesque laoreet, tortor
            malesuada volutpat luctus, augue diam venenatis
            risus</p>
        </div>
    </li>
    <li>
        <h3 class="uk-accordion-title"> Cloud</h3>
        <div class="uk-accordion-content">
```

```
            <p>Lorem ipsum dolor sit amet, consectetur
            adipiscing elit. Nam fermentum justo urna. Nam
            blandit diam ac erat congue, ullamcorper vulputate
            odio tempus. Quisque maximus dolor sit amet nisi
            lacinia euismod. Pellentesque laoreet, tortor
            malesuada volutpat luctus, augue diam venenatis
            risus</p>
        </div>
    </li>
    <li>
        <h3 class="uk-accordion-title"> Cloud</h3>
        <div class="uk-accordion-content">
            <p>Lorem ipsum dolor sit amet, consectetur
            adipiscing elit. Nam fermentum justo urna. Nam
            blandit diam ac erat congue, ullamcorper vulputate
            odio tempus. Quisque maximus dolor sit amet nisi
            lacinia euismod. Pellentesque laoreet, tortor
            malesuada volutpat luctus, augue diam venenatis
            risus</p>
        </div>
    </li>
</ul>
```

The example is the same as that of the previous accordion example; except here, you use the uk-accordion="multiple: true" property with the main <ul> tag.

The output of the code will show the first accordion open and the remaining closed. However, when you click the other two accordions, it will show the content without any of the accordions collapsing, as shown in Figure 4-22.

Cloud   −

Lorem ipsum dolor sit amet, consectetur adipiscing elit. Nam fermentum justo urna. Nam blandit diam ac erat congue, ullamcorper vulputate odio tempus. Quisque maximus dolor sit amet nisi lacinia euismod. Pellentesque laoreet, tortor malesuada volutpat luctus, augue diam venenatis risus

Cloud   −

Lorem ipsum dolor sit amet, consectetur adipiscing elit. Nam fermentum justo urna. Nam blandit diam ac erat congue, ullamcorper vulputate odio tempus. Quisque maximus dolor sit amet nisi lacinia euismod. Pellentesque laoreet, tortor malesuada volutpat luctus, augue diam venenatis risus

Cloud   −

Lorem ipsum dolor sit amet, consectetur adipiscing elit. Nam fermentum justo urna. Nam blandit diam ac erat congue, ullamcorper vulputate odio tempus. Quisque maximus dolor sit amet nisi lacinia euismod. Pellentesque laoreet, tortor malesuada volutpat luctus, augue diam venenatis risus

Figure 4-22. *Adding multiple accordions*

Icons

Finally, let's talk about icons in UIkit. If you remember the `<head>` section of the code examples, you use the following line of code:

```
<script src="https://cdnjs.cloudflare.com/ajax/libs/
uikit/3.0.0-beta.28/js/uikit-icons.min.js"></script>
```

This line is for the Scalable Vector Graphic icons, which are baked-in to UIkit. The best part of SVG icons is that they can be colored and styled with CSS to give an aesthetic look.

Listing 4-23 shows an example of a few icons used in UIkit.

Listing 4-23. Implementing Icons

```
<a href="" class="uk-margin-small-right" uk-icon="icon:
home"></a>
<a href="" class="uk-margin-small-right" uk-icon="icon:
trash"></a>
<a href="" class="uk-margin-small-right" uk-icon="icon:
users"></a>
<a href="" uk-icon="icon: phone"></a>

 <br><br><br><br>
<a href="" class="uk-icon-button uk-margin-small-right"
uk-icon="icon: twitter"></a>
```

```
<a href="" class="uk-icon-button  uk-margin-small-right"
uk-icon="icon: facebook"></a>
<a href="" class="uk-icon-button" uk-icon="icon: google-
plus"></a>
```

In Listing 4-23, you initially create the Home, Trash, Users, and Phone icons. For this, you use the <a> anchor tags with the href attribute. Then, you create the first icon (i.e., home) by using the property uk-icon="icon: home". As you can see, you assign the icon: home value to the uk-icon property. Similarly, you assign the trash value for the uk-icon for the trash using the uk-icon="icon: trash" property. You go on to create icons for users and the phone. You also use the uk-margin-small-right class for the spacing between the icons.

For social media button icons, you use the additional class uk-icon-button with the <a> tags. For the first social media icon button (i.e., Twitter), you use the uk-icon-button class followed by the uk-icon="icon: twitter" property. As you can see, the icon: twitter value is assigned to the uk-icon attribute. Similarly, you create the Facebook and Google Plus icons.

Figure 4-23 shows the output of the code.

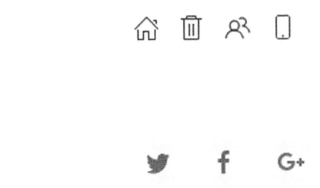

Figure 4-23. *Implementing icons*

Summary

As you learned in this chapter, UIkit is an expansive but light framework compared to heavyweights such as Bootstrap and Foundation. In the next chapter, you will learn about Material Design Lite, which is another amazing and intuitive framework.

CHAPTER 5

Material Design Lite Explained

Material Design Lite is an intuitive and lightweight framework compared to Bootstrap, Materialize, and Foundation. It adheres to the Material Design language launched by Google. MDL has ingrained UI Components that are easy to use and implement. It provides the styling and animations that help in constructing aesthetic and responsive web sites. It takes into consideration several aspects such as browser portability and responsiveness, all within a compact footprint.

Material Design, created by Google, is a design philosophy that is inspired by real materials and helps create sleek and interactive web sites. It follows Google's device-agnostic paradigm and stresses the need for web sites to look the same irrespective of the platform. In other words, it creates a uniformity across all devices, whether it's a tablet or a phone or a laptop. This is a distinct concept that helps create a consistent and unified experience that gives a real-world look and is aesthetically pleasing.

MDL is a unique framework with ample UI components, based on the Material Design philosophy. Though it may not possess a wide array of components compared to frameworks such as Bootstrap, it is quite resourceful and competent in its own way and provides a plethora of combinations and features to build responsive web sites. The name "Lite"

© Aravind Shenoy and Anirudh Prabhu 2018
A. Shenoy and A. Prabhu, *CSS Framework Alternatives*,
https://doi.org/10.1007/978-1-4842-3399-3_5

in this framework means it caters to the web designer's need to build immersive web sites in a lightweight manner, without the bulk or clutter associated with massive frameworks.

Installing MDL

MDL can be downloaded in several ways. One of the easiest ways is to go to `https://getmdl.io/started/index.html#download`. You will see a Download MDL button, as shown in Figure 5-1.

***Figure 5-1.** Download link for MDL*

Click the button to download a zipped file containing the various CSS and JavaScript files. Figure 5-2 shows the tree structure of the unzipped components.

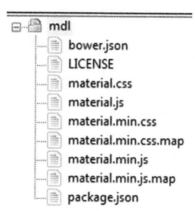

***Figure 5-2.** Structure of files in MDL*

The preferred way of including MDL in your document is to use the CDN links for the icons, CSS, and JavaScript files, as shown here:

```
<link rel="stylesheet" href="https://fonts.googleapis.com/
icon?family=Material+Icons">
<link rel="stylesheet" href="https://code.getmdl.io/1.3.0/
material.indigo-pink.min.css">
<script defer src="https://code.getmdl.io/1.3.0/material.min.js">
</script>
```

Just include the three lines of the preceding code in your HTML page and you are good to go. We already defined the advantages of using CDN links in the previous chapters, and the creators of MDL also recommend using the CDN links.

Alternatively, you can download and build MDL from the GitHub portal or by using Node or Bower.

In this chapter, we will stick to showing the preferred way (in other words, using CDN-hosted files in your markup file) to demonstrate various examples.

MDL Layout

In this section, you will look at some of the layout components of MDL so you can understand the MDL grid and other important attributes such as the footer and the tabs.

Initially, you will look at the header and drawer concepts in MDL by way of some simple examples.

Listing 5-1 shows a fixed header and a normal drawer in MDL.

Listing 5-1. Fixed Header with Normal Drawer in MDL

```
<html>
<head>
<link rel="stylesheet" href="https://fonts.googleapis.com/
icon?family=Material+Icons">
<link rel="stylesheet" href="https://code.getmdl.io/1.3.0/
material.indigo-pink.min.css">
<script defer src="https://code.getmdl.io/1.3.0/material.min.js">
</script>
</head>
<body>
 <div class = "mdl-layout mdl-js-layout mdl-layout--fixed-
   header">
          <header class = "mdl-layout__header">
            <div class = "mdl-layout__header-row">
                <!-- Title -->
                <span class = "mdl-layout-title">SUPERMAI
                              L007</span>
                <!-- Add spacer, to align navigation to the
                 right -->
                <div class = "mdl-layout-spacer"></div>
                <!-- Navigation -->
                <nav class = "mdl-navigation">
                   <a class = "mdl-navigation__link" href = ""
                      style = "color:white">INBOX</a>
                   <a class = "mdl-navigation__link" href = ""
                      style = "color:white">SPAM</a>
                   <a class = "mdl-navigation__link" href = ""
                      style = "color:white">TRASH</a>
                </nav>
             </div>
          </header>
```

```
<div class = "mdl-layout__drawer">
    <span class = "mdl-layout-title">SUPERMAIL007</span>
    <nav class = "mdl-navigation">
       <a class = "mdl-navigation__link"
         href = "">INBOX</a>
       <a class = "mdl-navigation__link"
         href = "">SPAM</a>
                   <a class = "mdl-navigation__link"
                     href = "">TRASH</a>
    </nav>
</div>

<main class = "mdl-layout__content">
    <div class = "page-content">Come Undone</div>
</main>
</div>

</body>
</html>
```

In Listing 5-1, you can see the code for the fixed header and a normal drawer. Let's look at each line of code to understand how it works.

In the head section, you include all the CDN files for the MDL framework. Then, you create a body tag in which you will define the functional markup for the fixed header example.

Then, you code a <div> and assign the mdl-layout, mdl-js-layout, and mdl-layout--fixed-header classes to it. The mdl-layout class identifies the container as an MDL component and is part of the outer container element. The mdl-js-layout class adds MDL behavior to the layout and is part of the outer container element. The mdl-layout--fixed-header class makes the header always visible, even on small screens.

Then, you define the HTML `<header>` tag wherein you assign the `mdl-layout__header` class to it. The assigned class identifies the container as an MDL component. Within the `<header>` tag, you code a `<div>` and assign the `mdl-layout__header-row` class to it. The `mdl-layout__header-row` class identifies the container as an MDL header row and is mandatory on a header content container. Inside the `<div>`, you create a `<span>` tag and assign the `mdl-layout-title` class to it that identifies the layout title text and that is needed on the layout title container. You use SUPERMAIL007 as the title content for the header. You then code another `<div>` to which you assign the `mdl-layout-spacer` class, which results in filling the remaining space and is usually used to align the elements to the right.

Then, you create the navigation element with the `<nav>` tag and assign the `mdl-navigation` class to it, which identifies the container as an MDL navigation group. You create three anchor links using the `<a>` tag and assign the `mdl-navigation__link` class that identifies the anchor as an MDL navigation link. You then use the words INBOX, SPAM, and TRASH as the content for the anchor tags. You complete this header section with a closing `<header>` tag.

Continuing, you create a `<div>` element and assign the `mdl-layout__drawer` class to it, which identifies the container as an MDL drawer. Then, you create a `<span>` element within that `<div>` and assign the `mdl-layout-title` class to it, which identifies the title text to the container. You use the content SUPERMAIL007, which is the same as the content for the header title in the `<header>` section. Then, you create the navigation element with the `<nav>` tag and assign the `mdl-navigation` class to it, which identifies the container as an MDL navigation group. You create three anchor links using the `<a>` tag and assign the `mdl-navigation__link` class to it, which identifies the anchor as an MDL navigation link. You then use the words INBOX, SPAM, and TRASH as the content for the anchor tags.

Next, you create a `<main>` tag to define the layout's primary content and assign the `mdl-layout__content` class to it. The `mdl-layout__content` class is mandatory for defining the container as the MDL layout content.

You then use the closing tags.

Figure 5-3 shows the code output.

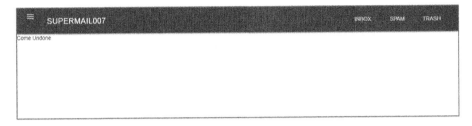

Figure 5-3. *Output of the fixed header and a normal drawer*

As you can see, you have created a fixed header that is visible on smaller screens too.

In addition, when you click the navicon (i.e., the menu icon), the drawer slides out, as shown in Figure 5-4.

Figure 5-4. *Drawer slides showing the content*

For a fixed drawer, all you need to do is to introduce the `mdl-layout-`
`-fixed-drawer` class to the first `<div>` within which the whole functional
markup is defined. The `<div>` line of code looks like this:

```
<div class = "mdl-layout mdl-js-layout mdl-layout--fixed-drawer
mdl-layout--fixed-header">
```

Figure 5-5 shows the output of the code.

Figure 5-5. *Fixed drawer*

Suppose you want a scrollable header that scrolls with the content.
In such a scenario, you can remove the `mdl-layout--fixed-header` class
from the first parent `<div>`. In the `<header>` tag, you need to introduce the
`mdl-layout__header–scroll` class. The rest of the code is the same, except
that you need to put comprehensive content within the layout content
`<main>` tag. The output will be similar, but when you scroll, the header will
not be fixed but will scroll with the content. Kindly refer to the code bundle
for the entire code and output.

In Listing 5-2, you will look at the code for a fixed header with
scrollable tabs.

Listing 5-2. Fixed Header with Scrollable Tabs

```
<div class = "mdl-layout mdl-js-layout mdl-layout--fixed-
header">
        <header class = "mdl-layout__header">
          <!-- Top row, always visible -->
```

```
    <div class = "mdl-layout__header-row">
       <!-- Title -->
       <span class = "mdl-layout-title">SUPERMAIL007
        </span>
    </div>

    <!-- Tabs -->
    <div class = "mdl-layout__tab-bar mdl-js-ripple-
     effect">
       <a href = "#scroll-tab-1" class = "mdl-layout__
        tab is-active">INBOX</a>
       <a href = "#scroll-tab-2" class = "mdl-layout__
        tab">SPAM</a>
       <a href = "#scroll-tab-3" class = "mdl-layout__
        tab">TRASH</a>
    </div>
</header>

<div class = "mdl-layout__drawer">
    <span class = "mdl-layout-title">SUPERMAIL007
     </span>
    <nav class = "mdl-navigation">
       <a class = "mdl-navigation__link"
        href = "">INBOX</a>
       <a class - "mdl-navigation__link"
        href = "">SPAM</a>
       <a class = "mdl-navigation__link"
        href = "">TRASH</a>
    </nav>
</div>
```

```
<main class = "mdl-layout__content">
  <section class = "mdl-layout__tab-panel is-active"
   id = "scroll-tab-1">
     <div class = "page-content"> Lorem ipsum dolor
      sit amet... (content) </div>
  </section>
  <section class = "mdl-layout__tab-panel" id =
   "scroll-tab-2">
     <div class = "page-content"> Lorem ipsum dolor
      sit amet, ...(content)</div>
  </section>
  <section class = "mdl-layout__tab-panel" id =
   "scroll-tab-3">
     <div class = "page-content"> Lorem ipsum dolor
      sit amet....(content) </div>
  </section>
</main>
</div>
```

In Listing 5-2, you define the parent `<div>` and assign the mdl-layout, mdl-js-layout, and mdl-layout--fixed-header classes to it. You then create a `<header>` tag to which you assign the mdl-layout__header class. Then, you create another `<div>` within the `<header>` tags to which you assign the mdl-layout__header-row class. You proceed to code a `<span>` tag to which you assign the mdl-layout-title class. You define the title content as SUPERMAIL007.

Next, you create the tabs. You create a `<div>` element to which you assign the mdl-layout__tab-bar and mdl-js-ripple-effect classes. The mdl-layout__tab-bar class identifies the container as an MDL tab bar, whereas the mdl-js-ripple-effect class is used for the immersive ripple effect. You then create three anchor links to which you assign the #scroll-tab-1, #scroll-tab-2, and #scroll-tab-3 href attributes, respectively.

You also assign the `mdl-layout__tab` classes to each anchor link. In the first anchor link, you assign the `is-active` class because it should be active by default. Use the `<header>` closing tag to wrap up this section of the code.

You then proceed to create a drawer similar to the example in Listing 5-1.

Next, you define the layout content within the `<main>` tags and assign the `mdl-layout__content` class to the `<main>` tag. You then create the first `<section>` tag and assign the `mdl-layout__tab-panel` class to it. Only for this `<section>` tag, you introduce the `is-active` class. Then you assign an ID whose value is the href attribute to the first anchor tag created in the `<header>` tag (i.e., `scroll-tab-1`). Next, you create a `<div>` and assign the page content class to it and define the content.

Similarly, you create two more sections similarly, the only difference being the ID assigned to them. You assign `scroll-tab-2` and `scroll-tab-3` as the value of the ID for the second and third sections, respectively.

Moving forward, you complete the code with the necessary closing tags. Figure 5-6 shows the output of the code.

Figure 5-6. *Output of scrollable tabs*

(We have used random content of `Lorem Ipsum...` in the code to illustrate this example, for the entire code with the massive content, refer to the code bundle for this chapter.)

Next, you will learn about the grid system in MDL. The grid system in MDL is quite easy and helps lay out the content for multiple devices based on different screen sizes. By default, a grid in MDL has 12 columns for the desktop screen, 8 for tablets, and 4 for phone sizes, and cells are laid out sequentially in a row.

As written on the MDL web site, there are two exceptions in MDL grid system.

- If a cell doesn't fit in the row in one of the screen sizes, it flows into the following line.

- If a cell has a specified column size equal to or larger than the number of columns for the current screen size, it takes up the entirety of its row.

Listing 5-3 shows the code sample for a grid layout.

Listing 5-3. Grid Layout

```
<div class="mdl-grid">
  <div style="text-align:center; border: 1px solid black;"
  class="mdl-cell mdl-cell--1-col">Cloud</div>
  <div style="text-align:center; border: 1px solid black;"
  class="mdl-cell mdl-cell--1-col">Cloud</div>
  <div style="text-align:center; border: 1px solid black;"
  class="mdl-cell mdl-cell--1-col">Cloud</div>
  <div style="text-align:center; border: 1px solid black;"
  class="mdl-cell mdl-cell--1-col">Cloud</div>
  <div style="text-align:center; border: 1px solid black;"
  class="mdl-cell mdl-cell--1-col">Cloud</div>
  <div style="text-align:center; border: 1px solid black;"
  class="mdl-cell mdl-cell--1-col">Cloud</div>
  <div style="text-align:center; border: 1px solid black;"
  class="mdl-cell mdl-cell--1-col">Cloud</div>
  <div style="text-align:center; border: 1px solid black;"
  class="mdl-cell mdl-cell--1-col">Cloud</div>
  <div style="text-align:center; border: 1px solid black;"
  class="mdl-cell mdl-cell--1-col">Cloud</div>
```

```
  <div style="text-align:center; border: 1px solid black;"
   class="mdl-cell mdl-cell--1-col">Cloud</div>
  <div style="text-align:center; border: 1px solid black;"
   class="mdl-cell mdl-cell--1-col">Cloud</div>
  <div style="text-align:center; border: 1px solid black;"
   class="mdl-cell mdl-cell--1-col">Cloud</div>
</div>
<div class="mdl-grid">
  <div style="text-align:center; border: 1px solid black;"
   class="mdl-cell mdl-cell--4-col">Cloud</div>
  <div style="text-align:center; border: 1px solid black;"
   class="mdl-cell mdl-cell--4-col">Cloud</div>
  <div style="text-align:center; border: 1px solid black;"
   class="mdl-cell mdl-cell--4-col">Cloud</div>
</div>
<div class="mdl-grid">
  <div style="text-align:center; border: 1px solid black;"
   class="mdl-cell mdl-cell--6-col mdl-cell--8-col-tablet">6 (8
   tablet)</div>
  <div style="text-align:center; border: 1px solid black;"
   class="mdl-cell mdl-cell--4-col mdl-cell--6-col-tablet">4 (6
   tablet)</div>
  <div style="text-align:center; border: 1px solid black;"
   class="mdl-cell mdl-cell--2-col mdl-cell--4-col-phone">2 (4
   phone)</div>
</div>
```

Listing 5-3 uses the following classes:

- mdl-grid: Identifies the <div> as an MDL grid
  component

- mdl-cell: Identifies the <div> as an MDL cell

- `mdl-cell--1-col`: Sets the column size for the cell to 1 cell of the 12 cells on a desktop screen

- `mdl-cell--4-col`: Sets the column size for the cell to 4 cells of the 12 cells on a desktop screen

- `mdl-cell--8-col-tablet`: Sets the column size for the cell to 8 cells on a tablet screen

- `mdl-cell--6-col-tablet`: Sets the column size for the cell to 6 cells on a tablet screen

- `mdl-cell--4-col-phone`: Sets the column size for the cell to 4 cells on a phone screen

If you see the code, you have used the `mdl-grid` class for the first parent `<div>`. You move on to create 12 child `<div>`s for 12 cells, and you use inline CSS styles for the borders of each cell. You assign `mdl-cell` and `mdl-cell--1-col` to each cell in the code, defining a total of 12 cells.

Next, you create another parent `<div>`, and similar to the first `<div>`, you assign the `mdl-grid` class to it. Then, you create three child `<div>` cells and assign `mdl-cell` and `mdl-cell--4-col` classes for it.

In the next parent `<div>`, you create a grid with three cells and define screen sizes for each child `<div>` cell by customizing the size of each cell on the default desktop, tablet, and phone.

Figure 5-7 shows the output of the code.

Figure 5-7. *Grid system sample in MDL*

Now that you have gained insight into some of the components of MDL, let's look at an example: how to build a web page with MDL.

Building an Intuitive Web Page Using MDL

In this section, you will take a look at the process of building a web page for Anirudh Prabhu, co-author of this book. It is a simple example. We will divide it into several steps and then apply the finishing touches to create an aesthetic page.

Step 1: Creating the <head> Section

Listing 5-4 shows step 1, wherein you create the <head> section of the web page and include all the JavaScript and CSS files.

Listing 5-4. <head> Section with All the JavaScript and CSS Files

```
<!DOCTYPE html>
<html>
<head>
        <meta charset="UTF-8">
        <title>Website Using Material Design Lite</title>
        <meta name="viewport" content="width=device-width,
         initial-scale=1">
        <link rel='stylesheet prefetch' href='https://fonts.
         googleapis.com/css?family=Roboto:400,100,500,300italic,
         500italic,700italic,900,300'>
        <link rel="stylesheet" href="https://code.getmdl.
         io/1.3.0/material.brown-orange.min.css" />
        <link rel='stylesheet prefetch' href='https://fonts.
         googleapis.com/icon?family=Material+Icons'>
        <link rel="stylesheet" href="style.css">
</head>
<body>
```

```
<script src='https://storage.googleapis.com/code.getmdl.
io/1.0.6/material.min.js'></script>
<script src='http://cdnjs.cloudflare.com/ajax/libs/
jquery/2.1.3/jquery.min.js'></script>
</body>
</html>
```

In Listing 5-4, you include the viewport attribute and the MDL files. You also add a custom style sheet, i.e., style.css.

Step 2: Creating a Fixed Header with a Drawer

In this section, you will add a code snippet between the <body> tags wherein you will define a fixed header and the header tile along with the drawer. See Listing 5-5.

Listing 5-5. Defining a Fixed Header and the Header Tile Along with the Drawer

```
<div class="mdl-layout mdl-js-layout mdl-layout--fixed-header
mdl-layout--fixed-tabs">
  <header class="mdl-layout__header">
    <div class="mdl-layout__header-row">
      <!-- Title -->
      <span class="mdl-layout-title">Anirudh Prabhu</span>
    </div>
    <!-- Tabs -->
    <div class="mdl-layout__tab-bar mdl-js-ripple-effect">
      <a href="#fixed-tab-1" class="mdl-layout__tab is-
      active">About</a>
      <a href="#fixed-tab-2" class="mdl-layout__tab">Moments</a>
    </div>
  </header>
```

```
<div class="mdl-layout__drawer">
  <span class="mdl-layout-title">Anirudh Prabhu</span>
  <div class="avatar">
    <img src="https://s3-us-west-2.amazonaws.com/s.cdpn.
    io/234228/cat.jpg" alt="Kaptain Kitty" class="avatar-img">
  </div>
  <!-- /.avatar -->

  <div class="drawer-text">
    Lorem ipsum dolor sit amet, consectetur adipisicing elit.
    Aspernatur officiis animi, soluta ab deserunt dolore
    fugit voluptatem laboriosam, magni. Eligendi quia quasi
    qui cupiditate optio fugit vel, suscipit harum illum.
  </div>
  <!-- /.drawer-text -->
</div>
<!-- /.mdl-layout__drawer -->
```

In Listing 5-5, initially, you define the <div> element to which you assign the mdl-layout, mdl-js-layout, mdl-layout--fixed-header, and mdl-layout--fixed-tabs classes. Then, you define the <header> tag to which you assign the mdl-layout__header class. Within the <header> tags, you create another <div> to which you assign the mdl-layout__header-row class, followed by creating a <span> element where you define the layout title using the mdl-layout-title class. Close the <div> tag and code another <div> for the fixed tabs to which you assign the mdl-layout__tab-bar and mdl-js-ripple-effect classes. Once you define the name of the tabs and close the concluding </header> tag, you define the code for the drawer.

You code a <div> and assign the mdl-layout__drawer class to it. You create the layout title for the drawer and then code another <div> to which you assign a custom avatar class. Then you introduce an image with the help of the <img> tags. Next you code another <div>, and you define the content for the drawer text.

Next, you define the custom CSS styles in the style.css file, as shown Listing 5-6.

Listing 5-6. Defining the Custom CSS styles

```
.mdl-layout__drawer-button,
.mdl-layout__drawer-button i {
  color: white;
}
@media (max-width: 900px) {
  .mdl-layout__drawer-button {
    width: 100%;
    margin: 0;
    background-color: transparent;
  }
}
img {
  max-width: 100%;
  height: auto;
  display: block;
}
.avatar {
  height: 200px;
  width: 200px;
  margin: 0 auto 2em;
}
.avatar-img {
  height: 200px;
  width: 200px;
  margin: 0 auto;
  border-radius: 50%;
}
```

```
.drawer-text {
  padding: 1em;
  text-align: center;
}
```

In Listing 5-6, you define the color of the drawer button as white and define the background color for it. Then, you define the style for the image, i.e., the maximum width along with the height and display attributes. You define the styles for the avatar class and for the avatar-img classes, in other words, for the height, width, and margin (and the border radius for the image). Finally, you use custom styles to center the drawer text.

Figure 5-8 shows the output of the code.

Figure 5-8. *Output of a header and drawer*

If you click the navicon to display the sliding drawer, you can see the drawer image and content, as shown in Figure 5-9.

Figure 5-9. *Sliding drawer content*

Step 3: Creating the About Section

You will now define the content for the About section, as shown in Listing 5-7.

Listing 5-7. About Section Code

```
<main class="mdl-layout__content">

    <div class="mdl-layout__tab-panel is-active" id="fixed-
    tab-1">
      <div class="page-content">
        <!-- Your content goes here -->
        <!-- Hero section -->
        <div class="hero-section">

          <div class="hero-text mdl-typography--text-center">

            <h1 class="mdl-typography--display-2">I'm Anirudh
            Prabhu</h1>
            <p class="mdl-typography--display-1">
              I'm a passionate mobile photographer
            </p>

            <a class="mdl-button mdl-js-button mdl-button--fab
            mdl-js-ripple-effect mdl-button--accent kitty-
            hero__text-button" href="#intro">
              <i class="material-icons">keyboard_arrow_down</i>
            </a>

          </div>
          <!-- /.hero-text -->

        </div>
        <!-- /.hero-section -->
```

```
<!-- INTRO -->
<div id="intro" class="mdl-grid intro-section">
  <div class="about-kitty mdl-cell mdl-cell--12-col">
    <p class="mdl-typography--headline">
      Welcome to my web page! I wish to display my
      mobile photography thru this web page.
    </p>
  </div>
  <!-- /.about-kitty -->

  <div class="about-kitty mdl-cell mdl-cell--12-col">
    <p>
      Various mobiles and gadgets with which i have
      performed photography.
    </p>
  </div>
  <!-- /.about-kitty -->

  <div class="about-kitty mdl-cell mdl-cell--5-col mdl-
   cell--1-col-tablet mdl-cell--hide-phone">
    <div class="circle-container">
      <div class="circle"></div>
      <div class="circle"></div>
      <div class="circle"></div>
    </div>
    <!-- /.circle-container -->

  </div>
  <!-- /.about-kitty -->
  <div class="about-kitty mdl-cell mdl-cell--7-col mdl-
   cell--6-col-tablet mdl-cell--4-col-phone">
    <div class="topics-container">
      <div class="topic">Xiaomi MI3</div>
```

```
            <div class="topic">OnePlus 2</div>
            <div class="topic">Sony DSC QX100</div>
        </div>
        <!-- /.topics-container -->
    </div>
  </div>
  <!--/.mdl-grid -->

  <!--/.mdl-grid -->

</div>
<!-- /.page-content -->

</main>
<!-- /.mdl-layout__content -->
```

In Listing 5-7, you code a `<main>` tag to which you assign the
`mdl-layout__content` class. You create a `<div>` and assign the
`mdl-layout__tab-panel` and `is-active` classes to it. You also assign an
ID of `fixed-tab-1` to it, which is the `href` attribute for the anchor tag for
the About section content. Within this, you code another `<div>` to define
the page content. You create another section within and assign the custom
class `hero-section` to it. Within this, you create another `<div>` to which
you assign the custom `hero-text` class along with the `mdl-typography-`
`-text-center` class. This centers the text. You then define the content
using different typography classes such as `mdl-typography--display-2`
and `mdl-typography--display-1`, which decides the font weight of the
content.

Next, you create a button, a circular one also called the *fab button*,
by defining the `mdl-button`, `mdl-js-button`, `mdl-button—fab`, `mdl-js-`
`ripple-effect`, and `mdl-button—accent` classes to define the look of the
button. You used a drop-down MDL arrow and embed it in the button.

After the `hero` section, you define a new parent `<div>` and assign the grid functionality to it. You then define the content for this introduction section. You define the `mdl-cell mdl-cell--12-col` class to it so that the content occupies 12 columns on a desktop. After you jot down the content, you then create three circles by using `mdl-cell`, `mdl-cell--5-col`, `mdl-cell--1-col-tablet`, and `mdl-cell--hide-phone`. This defines the cells based on the screen size such as tablets and phone, especially `mdl-cell--hide-phone`, which hides the content on a small phone. Next, you create the topic container section wherein you define the content that will eventually be placed next to the circles.

Now you create custom styles for the section, as shown in Listing 5-8.

Listing 5-8. Custom Styles

```
.hero-section {
  height: 100vh;
  /* IE11 doesn't like min-height */
  width: 100%;
  margin: 0;
  padding: 0;
  background-color: rgba(121,85,72, 0.6);
  background-image: -webkit-linear-gradient(rgba(121,85,72,
  0.3), rgba(121,85,72, 0.3)), url(https://pacdn.500px.
  org/2185509/e9a80e8a5bb01d46da6830d55a34c6c61146d27d/
  cover_2048.jpg?2);
  background-image: linear-gradient(rgba(121,85,72, 0.3),
  rgba(121,85,72, 0.3)), url(https://pacdn.500px.org/2185509/
  e9a80e8a5bb01d46da6830d55a34c6c61146d27d/cover_2048.jpg?2);
  background-position: center center;
  background-repeat: no-repeat;
  background-size: cover;
  position: relative;
```

```css
  display: -webkit-box;
  display: -ms-flexbox;
  display: flex;
  -webkit-box-orient: vertical;
  -webkit-box-direction: normal;
      -ms-flex-direction: column;
          flex-direction: column;
  margin: auto;
}

.hero-text {
  color: white;
  margin: auto;
}

@media screen and (max-width: 580px) {
  .hero-text p {
    white-space: pre-line;
  }
}

.kitty-hero__text-button, .mdl-button--fab.kitty-hero__text-
button {
  position: absolute;
  bottom: -28px;
  left: 50%;
  -webkit-transform: translateX(-50%);
          transform: translateX(-50%);
}

/* ABOUT KITTY INTRO + CARDS */

.intro-section,
.cards-section {
```

```css
  max-width: 960px;
}
/* ABOUT KITTY INTRO */

.intro-section, .mdl-grid.intro-section {
  padding: 5em 2em 5em;
}

.about-kitty p {
  max-width: 640px;
  margin: auto;
}

.circle-container {
  width: 100%;
  min-height: 100px;
  padding: 2em 0;
  display: -webkit-box;
  display: -ms-flexbox;
  display: flex;
  -webkit-box-orient: vertical;
  -webkit-box-direction: normal;
      -ms-flex-direction: column;
          flex-direction: column;
  -webkit-box-align: end;
      -ms-flex-align: end;
          align-items: flex-end;
}

.circle-container .circle {
  height: 16px;
  width: 16px;
  background-color: #c51162;
```

```
  border-radius: 50%;
  margin: 0 3px 9px;
}

.topics-container {
  padding: 2em 0;
}

.topics-container .topic {
  font-size: 20px;
  margin: 0 2px 5px;
}

@media screen and (max-width: 480px) {
  .topics-container .topic {
    margin-bottom: 0.5em;
  }
}
.embedded-img {
  max-width: 150px;
  max-height: 150px;
  margin: 0.5em;
  border-radius: 50%;
}
```

In the custom style sheet, you are essentially defining the background image, height, width, color, and flex characteristics for the hero section. You thereon define the text for the content with the custom hero-text class. You then define the maximum width of the intro-section followed by assigning the margin and padding for the paragraphs as well as for the element defined with the about-kitty class (which incidentally defines the circles and their respective topics). Next, you define the styles for the circle container and the subsequent circles. Moving forward, you define the styles for the topic container and topics along with the media query. Finally, you define the maximum width and height along with the border radius for the embedded image.

Figure 5-10 shows the output of the code.

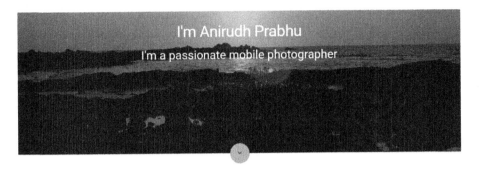

Figure 5-10. *Output of the About section*

Step 4: Inserting an Image with Content

Now you will develop both the About and Moments tabs, as shown in Listing 5-9.

Listing 5-9. Code for About and Moments Tabs

```
<!-- Testimonial -->
    <div class="mdl-grid mdl-grid--no-spacing fullwidth-
      panel">
      <div class="mdl-cell mdl-cell--12-col mdl-typography--
        text-center quote-panel">
        <blockquote>
```

```
      <p>
        Taking an image, freezing a moment, reveals how
        rich reality truly is.
      </p>
      <footer>
        – <cite>Anonymous</cite>
      </footer>
    </blockquote>

  </div>
  <!-- /.mdl-cell -->
</div>
<!--/.mdl-grid -->

</div>
<!-- /.page-content -->
</div>
<!-- /.tab1 -->
```

In Listing 5-9, you code a `<div>` and assign the `mdl-grid`, `mdl-grid-no-spacing`, and `fullwidth-panel` classes. While the `mdl-grid--no-spacing` class modifies the grid cells to have no margin between them, the `fullwidth-panel` class creates a panel that has a size of the entire grid. Within that `<div>`, you create another `<div>` and allocate a space of 12 columns using the `mdl-cell--12-col` class. You assign the typography class to the content and center the text. You also use the `quote-panel` styling for the content using the `quote-panel` class.

You then create a quote using the HTML `<blockquote>` tags.

Moving forward, you assign custom styles for the panel and insert a background image in the custom CSS style sheet, i.e., `style.css`, as shown in Listing 5-10.

Listing 5-10. Assigning Custom Styles

```
/* FULLWIDTH BACKGROUND SECTION */

.fullwidth-panel {
  color: white;
  background-color: rgba(156, 39, 176, 0.6);
}

.fullwidth-panel p {
  max-width: 640px;
  margin: auto;
}

.quote-panel {
  background-image: -webkit-linear-gradient(rgba(63, 81, 181,
  0.5), rgba(63, 81, 181, 0.5)), url('https://udemy-images.
  udemy.com/course/750x422/394968_538b_7.jpg');
  background-image: linear-gradient(rgba(63, 81, 181, 0.5),
  rgba(63, 81, 181, 0.5)), url('https://udemy-images.udemy.com/
  course/750x422/394968_538b_7.jpg');
  background-position: center 5%;
  background-repeat: no-repeat;
  background-size: cover;
  padding: 4em 2em 2em;
  display: -webkit-box;
  display: -ms-flexbox;
  display: flex;
  -ms-flex-line-pack: start;
      align-content: flex-start;
}

@media screen and (min-width: 800px) {
  .quote-panel {
    background-position: center 0;
```

```
      padding: 6em 2em;
  }
}

@media screen and (min-width: 1200px) {
  .quote-panel {
    background-position: center 8%;
    padding: 10em 2em 8em;
  }
}
```

In Listing 5-10, you assign the white color and define the background color to the section containing the fullwidth-panel class. You also define the maximum width and set an auto margin to it. Then, for the section pertaining to the quote-panel class, you insert a background image and define its position and size along with the padding. Using media queries, you assign the background position and padding for both the 800px and 1200px screen sizes.

Figure 5-11 shows the output of the code.

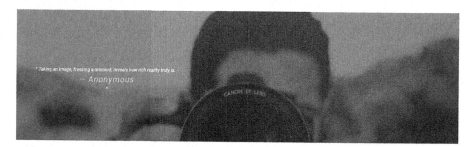

Figure 5-11. *Image with text*

Step 5: Developing the Content for the Moments Tab

Next, you will create the content for the second fixed tab, called Moments, which is next to the About fixed tab, as shown in Listing 5-11.

Listing 5-11. Code for Second Set of Fixed Tabs

```
<div class="mdl-layout__tab-panel" id="fixed-tab-2">
    <div class="page-content">
      <!-- Your content goes here -->

      <!-- CARDS  -->
      <div class="mdl-grid cards-section">
        <div class="mdl-cell mdl-cell--6-col mdl-cell--12-
          col-tablet mdl-card mdl-shadow--2dp home-bringing-
          card">
          <div class="mdl-card__title">
            <h2 class="mdl-card__title-text">Roses
              everywhere</h2>
          </div>
          <div class="mdl-card__supporting-text">
            Roses everywhere in flower market
          </div>
        </div>
        <!-- /.mdl-card -->
        <div class="mdl-cell mdl-cell--4-col mdl-cell--4-col-
          tablet mdl-cell--4-col-phone mdl-card mdl-shadow--
          2dp play-card">
          <div class="mdl-card__title">
            <h2 class="mdl-card__title-text">Random flower</h2>
          </div>
          <div class="mdl-card__supporting-text">
            Random flower
          </div>
        </div>

        <div class="mdl-cell mdl-cell--6-col mdl-cell--8-col-
          tablet mdl-cell--4-col-phone mdl-card mdl-shadow--
          2dp litter-card">
```

```
    <div class="mdl-card__title">
      <h2 class="mdl-card__title-text">Lilac</h2>
    </div>
    <div class="mdl-card__supporting-text">
      Lilacs are a beloved, fragrant shrub that produce
      clusters of light-purple flowers.
    </div>
  </div>
  <!--/.mdl-card -->
  <div class="mdl-cell mdl-cell--6-col mdl-cell--8-col-
    tablet mdl-cell--4-col-phone mdl-card mdl-shadow--
    2dp diet-card">
    <div class="mdl-card__title">
      <h2 class="mdl-card__title-text">Beautiful sunset
      at aguada beach</h2>
    </div>
    <div class="mdl-card__supporting-text">
      Beautiful sunset at aguada beach in Goa
    </div>
  </div>
  <!--/.mdl-card -->
  <!--/.mdl-card -->
</div>
<!--/.mdl-grid -->

</div>
<!-- /.page-content -->
</div>
```

In Listing 5-11, you define the content for the second fixed tab, called Moments.

Initially, you code a <div> and assign the grid class to it. You then jot down the code for four cards. For the first card, you use the mdl-card class and assign the space of 6 columns for the desktop and 12 columns for the tablet size using the mdl-cell, mdl-cell--6-col, and mdl-cell--12-col-tablet classes. Then, you define a shadow for aesthetics using the mdl-shadow--2dp class.

Next, you code a <div> and assign a title for the card using the mdl-card__title class. Thereon, you define the title text using the mdl-card__title-text class. Next, you assign the supporting content to the title using the mdl-card__supporting-text class.

Similarly, you create three more cards using different names for the content.

After you create the cards, you define custom styles in the custom style.css sheet, as shown in Listing 5-12.

Listing 5-12. Defining Custom Styles in the Custom style.css Sheet

```css
/* CARDS SECTION */

.cards-section {
  padding: 5em 0;
}

.mdl-card__title {
  min-height: 300px;
}
.mdl-card__title > .mdl-card__title-text {
  color: white;
}
```

```css
.home-bringing-card .mdl-card__title {
  background: -webkit-linear-gradient(rgba(0, 0, 0, 0.1), rgba
  (0, 0, 0, 0.8)), url('https://drscdn.500px.org/photo/210599845/
  q%3D80_h%3D300/v2?webp=true&sig=94f8683780d7d009224f477342bf4c34
  740920b5b75576cb8793ff52e7229b1a') center / cover;
  background: linear-gradient(rgba(0, 0, 0, 0.1), rgba(0, 0,
  0, 0.8)), url('https://drscdn.500px.org/photo/210599845/
  q%3D80_h%3D300/v2?webp=true&sig=94f8683780d7d009224f477342bf4
  c34740920b5b75576cb8793ff52e7229b1a') center / cover;
}

.play-card .mdl-card__title {
  background: url('https://drscdn.500px.org/photo/225478901/
  q%3D80_h%3D450/v2?webp=true&sig=ddd21866e9502c5f56aef387adf4c
  c0553513de4582ed30a5bc57ba817f43b06') center / cover;
}

.image-card {
  background: url('https://s3-us-west-2.amazonaws.com/s.cdpn.
  io/234228/image-card.jpg') center / cover;
}

.image-card > .mdl-card__actions {
  height: 52px;
  padding: 16px;
  background: rgba(0, 0, 0, 0.6);
}

.image-card__title {
  color: #fff;
  font-size: 14px;
  font-weight: 500;
}
```

```
.litter-card .mdl-card__title {
  background: -webkit-linear-gradient(rgba(0, 0, 0, 0.1),
  rgba(0, 0, 0, 0.8)), url('https://drscdn.500px.org/
  photo/187345183/q%3D80_h%3D450/v2?webp=true&sig=883a5a5734775
  d4b4084bd4f5fe7cd7ac9728bf0b6fc5d4ee91a522444023e6e') center
  / cover;
  background: linear-gradient(rgba(0, 0, 0, 0.1), rgba(0, 0,
  0, 0.8)), url('https://drscdn.500px.org/photo/187345183/
  q%3D80_h%3D450/v2?webp=true&sig=883a5a5734775d4b4084bd4f5fe7c
  d7ac9728bf0b6fc5d4ee91a522444023e6e') center / cover;
}

.diet-card .mdl-card__title {
  background: -webkit-linear-gradient(rgba(0, 0, 0, 0.1), rgba(0,
  0, 0, 0.8)), url('https://drscdn.500px.org/photo/109883725/
  q%3D80_h%3D450/v2?webp=true&sig=29611a8077b1b73ce190f28e138ed714
  7973317e15ba8c9ed418a4f797683df8') center / cover;
  background: linear-gradient(rgba(0, 0, 0, 0.1), rgba(0, 0,
  0, 0.8)), url('https://drscdn.500px.org/photo/109883725/
  q%3D80_h%3D450/v2?webp=true&sig=29611a8077b1b73ce190f28e138ed
  7147973317e15ba8c9ed418a4f797683df8') center / cover;
}

.card-small {
  min-height: auto;
}

.card-small > .mdl-card__title {
  color: rgba(0, 0, 0, 0.87);
  height: auto;
  min-height: auto;
}
```

```
.card-small .mdl-card__title-text {
  font-size: 16px;
}

.card-small .mdl-card__title-text:before {
  content: "";
  display: inline-block;
  margin-right: 0.5em;
  width: 18px;
  height: 18px;
  background-color: #c51162;
  border-radius: 50%;
}
```

In Listing 5-12, you assign the padding for the section containing the
cards-section class. You then define the minimum height and the white
color for the card title section. Thereon, you define the custom styles and
insert a background image for each of the four cards.

Moving on, you define the minimum height of the card for smaller
screens in addition to defining the color, height, and minimum height for
the smaller screen-sized cards and the section containing the card title.

You also define the font size, margins, height, background color, and
border radius for the styling of the cards on smaller screens, as well as the
title text.

Figure 5-12 shows the output of the code.

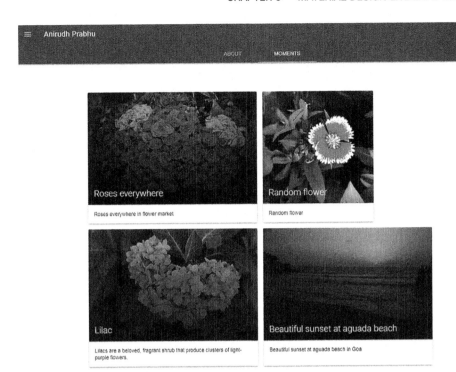

Figure 5-12. *Moments tab content*

Step 6: Designing the Footer Section

Finally, you will design a form and the footer section, as shown in Listing 5-13.

Listing 5-13. Form and the Footer Section

```
<!-- Contact -->
    <div class="mdl-grid mdl-grid--no-spacing">
      <!--/.contact-intro   -->

      <div class="mdl-cell mdl-cell--6-col mdl-cell--8-col-
        tablet mdl-cell--4-col-phone contact-panel form-panel
        mdl-color--brown-50">
```

```
      <form action="#">
        <div class="mdl-textfield mdl-js-textfield mdl-
          textfield--floating-label">
          <input class="mdl-textfield__input" type="text"
            id="name">
          <label class="mdl-textfield__label" for="name">Your
            name</label>
        </div>
        <div class="mdl-textfield mdl-js-textfield mdl-
          textfield--floating-label">
          <input class="mdl-textfield__input" type="email"
            id="email">
          <label class="mdl-textfield__label" for="email">
            Your email</label>
        </div>
        <div class="button-container clearfix">
          <button class="mdl-button mdl-js-button mdl-button-
            -raised mdl-js-ripple-effect mdl-button--accent
            subscribe-button">
            Join my fans
          </button>
        </div>
        <!--/.button-container -->
      </form>
    </div>
    <!--/.contact-panel -->

    <div class="mdl-cell mdl-cell--6-col mdl-cell--8-col-
      tablet mdl-cell--4-col-phone contact-panel address-panel
      mdl-typography--text-center mdl-color--brown-100">
```

```
    <p class="mdl-typography--title-color-contrast mdl-
     typography--text-nowrap mdl-typography--font-thin">
       <i class="material-icons">email</i> <a
        href="mailto:info@amp.com">info@amp.com</a>
    </p>

    <p class="mdl-typography--title-color-contrast mdl-
     typography--text-nowrap mdl-typography--font-thin">
       <a class="mdl-button mdl-js-button mdl-button--raised
        mdl-js-ripple-effect" href="twitter.com">twitter</a>
       <a class="mdl-button mdl-js-button mdl-button--
        raised mdl-js-ripple-effect" href="plus.google.
        com">Google+</a>
       <a class="mdl-button mdl-js-button mdl-button--raised
        mdl-js-ripple-effect" href="facebook.com">Facebook</a>
    </p>
  </div>
  <!-- /.contact-panel -->

</div>
<!-- /.mdl-grid -->

<!-- FOOTER -->
<footer class="mdl-mini-footer mdl-color--brown-200">
  <div class="mdl-mini-footer__left-section">
    <ul class="mdl-mini-footer__link-list">
      <li><a href="#">Help</a></li>
      <li><a href="#">Privacy & Terms</a></li>
    </ul>
  </div>
  <!-- /.mdl-mini-footer__left-section -->
</footer>
```

In Listing 5-13, you code a `<div>` and assign the grid class along with the no spacing class. You then define the space occupied by the grid columns on a tablet, phone, and desktop screen sizes. You assign custom classes to it so that you can use custom styles in the `style.css` sheet. You also assign the brown shade to this section using the `mdl-color--brown-50` class.

Moving forward, you define the form within the `<form>` tags. Inside the `<form>` tags, you create a `<div>` and assign `mdl-textfield`, `mdl-js-textfield`, and `mdl-textfield--floating-label` to design the text fields and use the MDL behavior for those fields. You create the Name and Email fields by adding the `mdl-textfield__input` to the input tag and `mdl-textfield__label` to the `<label>` tags apart from defining the type of the text fields.

You then create a button. First, you create a container for the button by using the `button-container` class. Then, you define another `<div>` element within that `<div>` and assign the `mdl-button`, `mdl-js-button`, `mdl-button—raised`, `mdl-js-ripple-effect`, and `mdl-button—accent` classes. This creates the button, assigns the `mdl` behavior, and creates the required effects and color to the button.

Then, you create a form. Once you are done with the form, you create the contact panel section to the right side of the form. You define another `<div>` and assign the column space for the cells depending on the screen size. You then define the typography, color contrast, and font using the `mdl-typography--title-color-contrast`, `mdl-typography--text-nowrap`, and `mdl-typography--font-thin` classes. Thereon, you define the e-mail icon using the `material-icons` class to the enclosed `<i>` tags. Then, you create another paragraph tags and create three anchor tags and define the button classes for the Twitter, Google+, and Facebook buttons using the `mdl-button`, `mdl-js-button`, `mdl-button—raised`, and `mdl-js-ripple-effect` classes.

Finally, you define the footer by using the <footer> tags to which you assign the mdl-mini-footer and mdl-color--brown-200 classes for the footer type due to which it will inherit the footer type and brown color. Within this section, you define the position of the footer using the mdl-mini-footer__left-section, which will align it to the left. You then define the link list using the <ul> and <li> tags.

Moving on, you define the custom styles for the preceding code, as shown in Listing 5-14.

Listing 5-14. Custom Styles for Listing 5-13

```
.contact-intro {
  color: rgba(255, 255, 255, 0.87);
}

.contact-panel {
  padding: 6em 4em;
  display: -webkit-box;
  display: -ms-flexbox;
  display: flex;
  -webkit-box-orient: vertical;
  -webkit-box-direction: normal;
      -ms-flex-direction: column;
          flex-direction: column;
  margin: auto;
}

.mdl-textfield {
  display: block;
  width: 100%;
  padding: 20px 0;
}
```

```css
@media screen and (min-width: 800px) {
  .subscribe-button {
    float: right;
  }
}

.address-panel {
  background-color: #dbdef1;
  color: rgba(255, 255, 255, 0.87);
}

.address-panel .material-icons {
  position: relative;
  top: 0.2em;
  display: inline-block;
  height: 30px;
  width: 30px;
  line-height: 30px;
  background-color: #ff4081;
  padding: 0.5em;
  border-radius: 50%;
}

.mdl-mini-footer,
.mdl-mini-footer .mdl-logo,
.mdl-mini-footer--link-list a,
.mdl-mini-footer__link-list a {
  color: rgba(0, 0, 0, 0.54);
}

ul {
  list-style-type: none;
}
```

```
/* UTILITIES */

.clearfix:after {
  content: "";
  display: table;
  clear: both;
}

.float-right {
  float: right;
}

.float-left {
  float: left;
}
```

In Listing 5-14, you define the color for the contact and assign the padding and display properties for the contact-panel section. You also define the display type, width, and padding for the text fields in the form. You shift the submit button of the form to the right of the form section. For the same button, you use the clearfix and float properties to automatically clear the child elements without using any additional markup. You move on to define the background color of the panel along with the panel color. You also define the position, height, inline block display, padding, and border radius for the material icons. You set the color to the logo and link list of the footer. You remove the listing bullets from the list using the list-style-type: none; property.

Figure 5-13 shows how the final page will look.

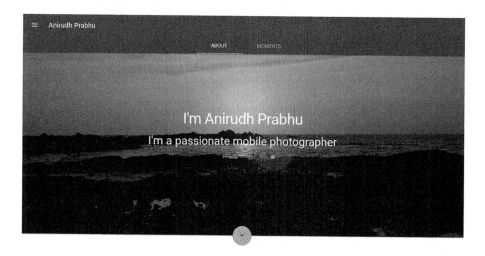

Welcome to my web page! I wish to display my mobile photography thru this web page.

Various mobiles and gadgets with which I have performed photography.

- Xiaomi MI3
- OnePlus 2
- Sony DSC QX100

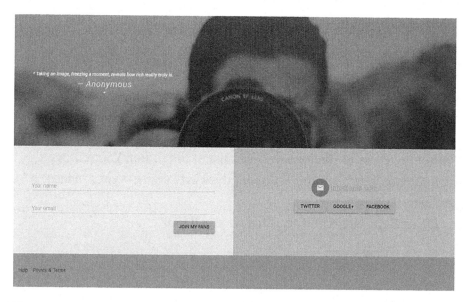

Figure 5-13. *Complete web page with the footer section*

Summary

In this chapter, you learned about the subtle nuances of the intuitive MDL framework. It is a lightweight framework and can help you design an interactive web site with ease. It is quite resourceful and is a vital cog in the wheel for small projects compared to heavyweight frameworks because it helps you build remarkable, immersive web pages. In the next chapter, you will look at the last light framework/utility covered in this book, called Susy.

CHAPTER 6

Susy Explained

So far, you have seen quite a few frameworks that can be used to make interactive web sites. We, as web designers, know that a grid layout is essential to position the elements effectively. Most frameworks, including the ones covered in this book, have a concept of a grid system.

Even though with Flex Grid and the CSS Grid module radically changing the dynamics of grid layouts, creating a layout can be quite a juggling act. Enter Susy- a lightweight utility for creating fast, responsive, and customizable grids that also helps keep the content and styling separate.

With Sass gaining ground in the world of web design, we have decided to give you an overview of this Sass-based framework that is used solely for building awesome grid layouts.

To understand Susy, you need to have at least a basic knowledge of Sass, but it's quite easy to learn Susy once you are through with that. The benefit of Susy (or any Sass-inspired framework) is that you can choose only the attributes you need, eliminating the need to include other properties.

© Aravind Shenoy and Anirudh Prabhu 2018
A. Shenoy and A. Prabhu, *CSS Framework Alternatives*,
https://doi.org/10.1007/978-1-4842-3399-3_6

It abstracts away the time-consuming nature of building complex grid layouts and allows you to focus on more important things in your core web design projects. It also allows you to fine-tune your grid layouts quickly instead of spending a lot of time on coding grids.

You will now learn how to create a 4×3 grid layout using Susy.

Creating a 4×3 Responsive Grid Layout

There are many ways to install Susy, but for this example, we will be using Node Package Manager (NPM) and a task runner called Grunt to get going.

We will walk you through each phase in this example. Follow these steps:

1. Create a project directory.

2. Execute the `npm init` command inside the created directory. This initializes a node project inside the directory and creates the necessary files and directories for executing the project. Refer to Figure 6-1.

```
    Terminal   Shell   Edit   View   Window   Help

Last login: Sat Nov 25 11:02:42 on console
Anirudhs-Mac-2:~ anirudhprabhu$ cd Documents/
Anirudhs-Mac-2:Documents anirudhprabhu$ ls
Build            Susytrain          materialize      susytraining
Anirudhs-Mac-2:Documents anirudhprabhu$ cd Susytrain/
Anirudhs-Mac-2:Susytrain anirudhprabhu$ npm init
This utility will walk you through creating a package.json file.
It only covers the most common items, and tries to guess sensible defaults.

See `npm help json` for definitive documentation on these fields
and exactly what they do.

Use `npm install <pkg>` afterwards to install a package and
save it as a dependency in the package.json file.

Press ^C at any time to quit.
package name: (susytrain)
version: (1.0.0)
description:
entry point: (index.js)
test command:
git repository:
keywords:
author:
license: (ISC)
About to write to /Users/anirudhprabhu/Documents/Susytrain/package.json:

{
  "name": "susytrain",
  "version": "1.0.0",
  "description": "",
  "main": "index.js",
  "scripts": {
    "test": "echo \"Error: no test specified\" && exit 1"
  },
  "author": "",
  "license": "ISC"
}


Is this ok? (yes)
Anirudhs-Mac-2:Susytrain anirudhprabhu$ ▊
```

Figure 6-1.   *Creating a project using npm init*

3. Install Susy through NPM using the following
    command:

```
npm install susy
```

However, if you are using a Linux or a Mac, you
need to use sudo to perform the installation. Since
in this example we are using a Mac, we will use the
following command:

```
sudo npm install susy
```

Figure 6-2 shows the terminal where we have entered this command.

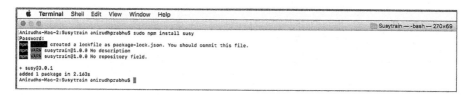

Figure 6-2. *Installation of Susy*

4. You will install a task runner (a build automation
    utility) called Grunt. Grunt is quite useful when
    you need to perform repetitive tasks such as
    minification, compilation, unit testing, and linting,
    to name a few. It simplifies the tasks to a great extent
    and is quite a nice toolkit in your arsenal for real-
    time web design projects.

    For the steps to install Grunt, refer to the following
    web site: https://gruntjs.com/installing-grunt.

```
npm install -save-dev grunt
```

5. Install the Sass plug-in for Grunt. This can be done
    with the following command:

```
npm install grunt-contrib-sass --save-dev
```

However, if you are using a Mac or Linux-based
system, you need to add sudo before the preceding
command, as shown in Figure 6-3.

Figure 6-3. *Installation of Sass plug-in for Grunt*

6. Create Gruntfile.js in the root directory of the
    project. This file needs to contain all the Grunt task
    runner information, as shown in Listing 6-1.

Listing 6-1. Configuration for Grunt Task Runner

```
module.exports = function(grunt) {

  // Project configuration.
  grunt.initConfig({
    sass: {
      dist: {
        options: {
          style: 'expanded',
          require: 'susy'
        },
        files: {
          'css/style.css': 'scss/style.scss'
        }
```

```
      }
    }
});

// Load the plugin that provides the "sass" task.
grunt.loadNpmTasks('grunt-contrib-sass');

// Default task(s).
grunt.registerTask('default', ['sass']);

};
```

Figure 6-4 shows the configuration in a text editor.

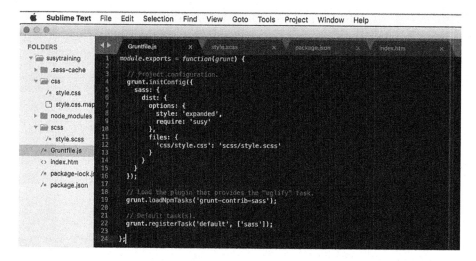

Figure 6-4. *Configuration for the Grunt Task Runner*

The grunt.initConfig section contains the Grunt
configuration necessary for the project. Next, you
load the Sass plug-in for Grunt needed for the
project from https://github.com/gruntjs/grunt-
contrib-sass.

You can follow the installation procedures for installing the Sass plug-in at the previously mentioned web site. After loading the plug-ins, you can define tasks that need to be automated. Refer to the same web site to see the detailed procedure.

7. Create your Sass file in the sass directory. For this project, you will create a 4×3 grid layout used typically for displaying a photo gallery. Listing 6-2 shows the HTML code for the grid.

Listing 6-2. Creating a 4×3 Grid

```html
<!DOCTYPE html>
<html>
<head>
  <title>Susy example</title>
  <meta name="viewport" content="width=device-width, initial-
  scale=1">
  <link rel="stylesheet" type="text/css" href="css/style.css">
</head>
<body>
<div class="container clearfix">
  <section>
    <ul class="blocks">
      <li class="block__item"></li>
      <li class="block__item"></li>
      <li class="block__item"></li>
      <li class="block__item"></li>
      <li class="block__item"></li>
      <li class="block__item"></li>
      <li class="block__item"></li>
      <li class="block__item"></li>
      <li class="block__item"></li>
```

```
    <li class="block__item"></li>
    <li class="block__item"></li>
    <li class="block__item"></li>
   </ul>
  </section>
 </div>
</body>
</html>
```

As you can see, we have created a list of 12 blocks and defined the style sheet for the code.

8. Define the Sass code in the file style.scss in the scss folder. The code for this file is shown in Listing 6-3. You begin by importing Susy into your Sass file by using the @import component of Sass. This is followed by defining the Susy configuration, which is specified in susy(). This configuration will contain values for a number of columns, gutters, maximum widths of the container, and so on. You then define colors and breakpoints for media queries using Sass variables. Moving forward, you define styles for the classes container and block_item. You use the mixins container(), gutter(), and gallery() that are available in the Susy framework. The container() mixin sets the container position to center along with the maximum width specified within the configuration. Similarly, gutter() sets the gutter space.

    The gallery() mixin is used to create the desired block layout. This mixin accepts the desired number of columns as a parameter.

Listing 6-3. Defining the Styles

```
@import "susy";

$susy: (
  columns: 12,
  gutters: 1/4,
  container: 71.25rem,
  global-box-sizing: border-box,
);

// Colours
$color-primary: #38a1d6;
$color-secondary: #16f4d0;
$color-tertiary: #fcee21;
$color-grey: #a1acb5;
$color-grey-light: #dce8ef;
$color-grey-dark: #333;

// Breakpoints
$mobile-landscape: 30rem; // 480px
$tablet: 40rem; // 640px
$tablet-wide: 48rem; // 768px
$desktop: 64rem; // 1024px
$widescreen: 71.25rem; // 1140px

* {
  box-sizing: border-box;
}

%clearfix {
  &:after {
    content: "";
```

```scss
    display: table;
    clear: both;
  }
}

body {
  padding: 0 .625rem;
}

.container {
  @include container();
}

section {
  @extend %clearfix;
  margin-bottom: gutter();
}

.block {
  margin: 0;
  @extend %clearfix;
}

.block__item {
  background-color: $color-tertiary;
  height: 8rem;
  margin-bottom: gutter();
  list-style: none;

  &:nth-last-child(-n+2) {
    margin-bottom: 0;
  }

  @media (min-width: $tablet) {
    @include gallery(4);
```

```
  &:nth-last-child(-n+3) {
    margin-bottom: 0;
  }
}

@media (min-width: $desktop) {
  @include gallery(3);

  &:nth-last-child(-n+4) {
    margin-bottom: 0;
  }
}
}
```

9. Run the Grunt file from the terminal in the root directory using the following command:

```
Grunt
```

10. The style.scss file compiles to style.css. Now when you click the HMTL file, you will see the output shown in Figure 6-5.

Figure 6-5. *Output of 4×3 grid*

If you resize the browser, then you will see that the grid behaves in a responsive way as defined in the code.

Also, if you check the `style.css` file created by compiling the `style.scss` Sass file, you can see the code shown in Listing 6-4.

Listing 6-4. Style.css

```css
* {
  box-sizing: border-box;
}

section:after, .block:after {
  content: "";
  display: table;
  clear: both;
}

body {
  padding: 0 .625rem;
}

.container {
  max-width: 71.25rem;
  margin-left: auto;
  margin-right: auto;
}
.container:after {
  content: " ";
  display: block;
  clear: both;
}

section {
  margin-bottom: 1.6949152542%;
}
```

```
.block {
  margin: 0;
}

.block__item {
  background-color: #fcee21;
  height: 8rem;
  margin-bottom: 1.6949152542%;
  list-style: none;
}
.block__item:nth-last-child(-n+2) {
  margin-bottom: 0;
}
@media (min-width: 40rem) {
  .block__item {
    width: 32.2033898305%;
    float: left;
  }
  .block__item:nth-child(3n + 1) {
    margin-left: 0;
    margin-right: -100%;
    clear: both;
    margin-left: 0;
  }
  .block__item:nth-child(3n + 2) {
    margin-left: 33.8983050847%;
    margin-right: -100%;
    clear: none;
  }
  .block__item:nth-child(3n + 3) {
    margin-left: 67.7966101695%;
    margin-right: -100%;
```

```
    clear: none;
  }
  .block__item:nth-last-child(-n+3) {
    margin-bottom: 0;
  }
}
@media (min-width: 64rem) {
  .block__item {
    width: 23.7288135593%;
    float: left;
  }
  .block__item:nth-child(4n + 1) {
    margin-left: 0;
    margin-right: -100%;
    clear: both;
    margin-left: 0;
  }
  .block__item:nth-child(4n + 2) {
    margin-left: 25.4237288136%;
    margin-right: -100%;
    clear: none;
  }
  .block__item:nth-child(4n + 3) {
    margin-left: 50.8474576271%;
    margin-right: -100%;
    clear: none;
  }
  .block__item:nth-child(4n + 4) {
    margin-left: 76.2711864407%;
    margin-right: -100%;
    clear: none;
```

```
  }
  .block__item:nth-last-child(-n+4) {
    margin-bottom: 0;
  }
}
/*# sourceMappingURL=style.css.map */
```

This is how the mixins and variables created in Sass were compiled to CSS code, helping you keep the content and styling separate.

Summary

In this chapter, you got an overview of Susy. With Susy, you can develop interactive and advanced grid layouts for your web designing projects. The learning curve of grids is steep, and the more you delve deep, you will realize that there is much more to learn. In a way, more is less (pun intended).

In this book we covered five frameworks that you can use instead of Bootstrap, Foundation, and Materialize. We stressed how these lightweight frameworks provide enough capability to design immersive web sites. However, this book was just an introduction to these frameworks. You are just on the shore of the island; the sea of knowledge is far beyond. In addition to these frameworks, there are several other user interface kits and web design toolkits that can make your web designing projects a breeze. Ideally, this book has helped you gain insight into the inner workings of these streamlined frameworks and whetted your appetite to go for more.

Keep learning!

Index

Get the eBook for only $5!

Why limit yourself?

With most of our titles available in both PDF and ePUB format, you can access your content wherever and however you wish—on your PC, phone, tablet, or reader.

Since you've purchased this print book, we are happy to offer you the eBook for just $5.

To learn more, go to http://www.apress.com/companion or contact support@apress.com.

Apress®

Printed by Printforce, the Netherlands